10

D0969271

BIGGEST
LIES

—OF THE—

ENEMY

AND HOW TO COMBAT THEM

10

THE

BIGGEST
LIES

—OF THE—

ENEMY

AND HOW TO COMBAT THEM

DEACON

Keith Strohm

Published by The Word Among Us Press
7115 Guilford Drive, Suite 100
Frederick, Maryland 21704
wau.org

22 21 20 19 18   1 2 3 4 5

ISBN: 978-1-59325-330-1
eISBN: 978-1-59325-505-3

Unless otherwise indicated, Scripture texts in this work are taken
from the *New American Bible, revised edition* © 2010, 1991, 1986, 1970
Confraternity of Christian Doctrine, Washington, D.C.
All rights reserved.

Scripture quotations marked RSVCE are from the *Revised Standard
Version of the Bible—Second Catholic Edition* (Ignatius Edition),
© 2006 National Council of the Churches of Christ in the
United States of America. All rights reserved.

Excerpts from the English translation of the *Catechism of the Catholic
Church* (CCC) for use in the United States of America, Second Edition,
copyright © 1997, by the United States Catholic Conference—Libreria
Editrice Vaticana. Used with permission.

Cover design by Faceout Studio

Made and printed in the United States of America.

Library of Congress Control Number: 2018934144

All the names and identifying circumstances of people in
the stories that appear in this book have been changed to protect
the privacy of individuals.

Acknowledgements

Far more goes into the creation of a book than an author's words.

Book publishing is a team sport, and I am surrounded by an amazing team, many of whom I have never met—yet that hasn't stopped them from pouring their passion, creativity, and technical talents into making this project a reality. This book would not have happened without the providential movement of the Holy Spirit, the prayer and discernment of The Word Among Us Press team, and especially the initiative of Beth McNamara, the publisher. Like any relationship, the collaboration between an author and a publishing team takes commitment, hard work, mutual respect, willingness to compromise, and a host of other qualities. Most times it works well; sometimes it doesn't. But every so often, in the mysterious workings of Divine Providence and human receptivity, that collaboration becomes something truly special, a real partnership.

This book is proof of that partnership.

So, I wanted to take this opportunity to offer my heartfelt thanks and appreciation for the entire staff of The Word Among Us Press—especially Jeff Smith, President; Beth McNamara, Publisher; Cindy Cavnar, my incredibly talented editor; and all of the marketing, sales, logistics, and administrative folks. Your efforts on behalf of this book are both humbling and deeply encouraging. The fruits that the Lord will bring forth from this book will be just as much a result of your collaboration as mine. I look forward to what the Lord does with this partnership in the future.

I would also be remiss if I didn't take a few moments to thank Kristen Bird, Executive Director of *Burning Hearts Disciples* and a close friend, colleague, and collaborator. A few weeks after signing the contract for this book, Kristen and I led a parish mission focusing on the lies of the Enemy. Her insight and ability to communicate the love of the Father were instrumental in shaping my approach to this project.

As usual, I'd also like to thank my gang of collaborators, especially Fr. Matt Bozovsky for his theological acumen, Bobby Vidal for sharing his expertise as well as insight into personal friendship with the saints, Rachel Espinoza for offering wise feedback on the manuscript based on her pastoral experience, and Fr. Jeffrey Grob of the Archdiocese of Chicago, colleague, mentor, and friend. Any errors in this text are purely my own. Also, I'd like to recognize my pastor, Fr. Fred Pesek, whose Christmas homily about being wrapped and swaddled influenced the imagery I used in this book.

Finally, I couldn't have written this book without the love, support, and sacrifice of my wise and patient wife, Debbie, and my amazing daughter, Siena. I treasure you both!

Every weapon fashioned against you shall fail;
every tongue that brings you to trial
you shall prove false.
This is the lot of the servants of the LORD,
their vindication from me. (Isaiah 54:17)

To Kristin Bird, Julianne Stanz,
and Sr. Marie Kolbe Zamora—
three amazing collaborators and sisters in
Christ who have challenged me to be a better
speaker, deacon, and disciple.

Contents

Introduction

*"You will know the truth, and the truth
will set you free." (John 8:32)*

I once heard a story that helped me to appreciate the dynamic between lies versus the truth. It went like this.

Twin brothers—a man named Truth and a man named Lie—stood by a river out in the country. Lie said he could swim across the river faster than Truth and challenged him to a race to prove it. They had to take off all their clothes, Lie said, dive in, and swim to the other side and back. Truth agreed, but when Lie shouted "On your mark, get set, go," Truth jumped in and Lie did not. With Truth out in the middle of the river, Lie put on Truth's clothes and headed into town where he paraded around dressed as Truth. When Truth returned to shore, Lie's clothes were there on the ground, but Truth refused to dress as Lie. Instead, he walked back to town naked. People stared and were offended when they saw him, even though he explained the situation and said that he was, in fact, Truth. But he made people uncomfortable and so they mocked and shunned him. They didn't believe he was really Truth. The people believed Lie because he looked good, he was dressed properly, and he was easier to take. From that day until this, people have come to believe a lie rather than believe a naked truth.

Lies have a particular ability to capture our attention. Whether someone has lied to us about a particular situation, lied about us to someone else, or whether we have, perhaps with good intentions, lied ourselves, we've all experienced the power of lies. Lies can influence how we see and react to others, interpret the world around us, and understand our own identity.

That's why lies are the devil's stock in trade. Even when the lie is ugly, we have a tendency to accept it more readily than the truth—particularly when it is aimed at our identity.

I should know. I was bound up and influenced by lies for over half my life. I "knew" that I was broken, that there was something about me that God couldn't love. In my head, I understood that God had created me and loved me in some sort of way. However, the lies wrapped around me were so strong that I couldn't live out of the truth of my identity as a beloved son of God.

Throughout my ministry in the Catholic world over the last twenty years, I have frequently encountered the same self-understanding in others—baptized men and women who don't live in the freedom, peace, joy, and integrity of their identity as sons and daughters of God, but rather struggle with a very real and pervasive bondage. For too many of us, God seems like a distant, unapproachable figure, and we struggle over and over again with the same sins, our sense of guilt deepening into an unshakeable experience of shame. Perhaps we are sure that God is a loving Father, but we are not too sure what this Father thinks of us. Or perhaps we suspect that the Father is anything but loving—majestic, omnipotent, all-seeing, all-judging, sure. But *tender*? *Intimate*? No way.

Even for those who have experienced some freedom in Jesus Christ, there are places in our lives that stubbornly resist the sovereign grace and love of the Father, areas that do not yield to the mercy and forgiveness offered by the Son, no matter how close to the sacraments we remain.

How can this be?

If the experience of baptism does accomplish something real and meaningful in us—and we believe it does—if the sacramental life of the Church really does have power to change us, then what gives? Why are so many of God's children bound by fear, brokenness, shame, and the uncertain, often traumatic circumstances of living in a fallen world? Looking at the situation through this lens, one would be tempted to believe that this experience of bondage, struggle, and lack of breakthrough in the spiritual life is just the way it is—perhaps intentionally so. In other words, we can easily conclude that life, for Christians, is purposely designed as a kind of lifelong Lent and the best we can hope for is to suffer through it with a flinty-eyed tenacity long enough to squeak into purgatory.

As we will see throughout this book, the lies of Satan influence us in many ways, but the Father has uttered a single response to the lies of the Enemy—the Word, who assumed our nature and became truth incarnate. At the heart of the Church's mission of evangelization and her ministry of reconciliation and healing is the proclamation and manifestation of this truth in the lives of all whom she encounters. Real and authentic freedom is a gift offered to every person by the Father in Jesus through the power of the Holy Spirit. It is not the purview of the extra-graced or the lucky. The Enemy's lies may bind us and blind us to who we really are in Christ, but they can never overcome the Father's love made manifest in Jesus. After all, it was this love that "delivered us from the power of darkness and transferred us to the kingdom of his beloved Son, in whom we have redemption, the forgiveness of sins" (Colossians 1:13-14).

So when Beth McNamara, publisher of The Word Among Us Press, attended a parish mission that I gave, and then suggested that I write this, I had to say yes. Helping others encounter Christ includes accompanying them on this journey through the minefield of lies laid out by Satan. The Lord has sent people in my own life to walk with me on a continuing journey of freedom, and I have spent my years in ministry doing that for others. In many ways, this book is a kind of field report of what I have seen and experienced, of both the Enemy's tactics and the enduring power of the Father's love to break every chain that binds his children.

Therefore, as you read, hold on to hope. There is a way through the Enemy's lies; there is a way that leads to true peace, joy, healing, and wholeness; there is a way to freedom from shame, anger, fear, and addiction. That way has a name, and that name is Jesus, who is The Way. My prayer is simply that this book would serve as an encounter with the One who is Truth, and in that encounter the kingdom of God and all of its transformative power would be released in your life.

Because the truth will set you free!

Chapter One

The Devil Is a Liar

*He was a murderer from the beginning
and does not stand in truth, because there is
no truth in him. (John 8:44)*

The devil *is* a liar.

Go ahead and read that sentence again. This time, notice the emphasis. The devil doesn't just tell lies. He is not just a spreader of false news or someone who avoids telling the truth to spare himself (and others) pain and embarrassment. He doesn't just lie as part of a larger overarching strategy of evil.

The devil lies because, in his rebellion against God, his very nature has become corrupted. He has totally rejected the One who is truth. Truth is absent in him. In a certain sense, therefore, we can say that his very identity--his very nature--is now a lie, and this nature is opposed to the nature of God. The Enemy despises God and the things of God—and particularly his children. He has set his thoughts, actions, and the power of his kingdom of lies against us, desiring most of all that, confused by the false testimony of darkness, we would abuse the gift of our free will and reject the Father's invitation to restoration, renewal, freedom, and new life.

Knowing the Enemy's work in human history, Jesus calls him the father of lies (John 8:44). This title is rooted in the very first lie in all of creation, which the Enemy uttered to Eve in the Garden of Eden. This is why Jesus also calls him a "murderer from the beginning." Because of that lie, Adam and Eve let trust in their Creator die in their hearts, and they chose themselves over God. As a result, sin, death, and suffering entered the world and have dominated human history.

Even though definitively defeated by Jesus in his passion, death, resurrection, and ascension, Satan continues to spin his web of lies, hoping to take as many people with him before the final manifestation of the kingdom of God when Jesus returns.

The Battlefield

The apostle Paul spent time spreading awareness of—and equipping his people for—this battle between Satan and the children of God. In his Letter to the Church at Ephesus, Paul wrote: "For our struggle is not with flesh and blood but with the principalities, with the powers, with the world rulers of this present darkness, with the evil spirits in the heavens" (6:12). Paul understood that in our quest for holiness and justice, we would face opposition not only from the natural order—the temptations, obstacles, and wounds that come from living in a world that is imperfect and itself wounded by the fall—but also from the supernatural realm. Principalities and powers in this passage refer to members of the hierarchy of fallen angels. Paul understands, therefore, that even though Jesus Christ has won the victory over Satan and his kingdom, the forces of that kingdom still oppose themselves against every believer and community, hoping to block the manifestation of that victory in our lives.

Since we are, indeed, in a battle, it is in our best interest to understand the battlefield. On a tactical level, knowing the geography of the landscape can provide a solid advantage in war. Scripture tells us that in the battle with the Enemy and his lies, our battlefield is largely in our heart.

Now, in our 21st century usage, the "heart" often signifies affections or emotions. The battle that we fight, however, is not primarily about feelings or emotionally-charged opinions. It goes much deeper. Scripturally, the heart refers to the center of the human person, the foundation of physical, emotional, intellectual, and moral activity. We may only see the surface appearance, Scripture says, but "the LORD looks into the heart" (1 Samuel 16:7). In this worldview, the heart is the place of deep thought, understanding, and moral choice.

There is another field of battle—the mind—and Scripture in many places uses the terms "heart" and "mind" interchangeably (they do take on more distinctive meanings as Christian understanding of revelation grows). In contemporary thought, however, the mind is seen only as the place of thinking, reasoning, or knowledge. But this battle with Satan is not just about knowing the right information or thinking about and believing the right kinds of doctrines. It is about a deep understanding of *who God is, who he is for us, and who we are in him.* In this way, the word "mind" functions in way that is very similar to "heart." Our purposes here, then, are best served in seeing the heart (and mind) as the inner reality of the human person that shape how we think, speak, act, and feel.

The heart, in this context, is the place of battle for us. It is from this place that our thoughts, choices, beliefs, and actions emerge. Jesus himself speaks to the importance of the heart.

After chastising the Pharisees and scribes for their tendency to place the demands of the Law and tradition before those who suffer, Jesus said to his disciples:

> Do you not realize that everything that goes into a person from outside cannot defile, since it enters not the heart but the stomach and passes out into the latrine? . . . But what comes out of a person, that is what defiles. From within people, from their hearts, come evil thoughts, unchastity, theft, murder, adultery, greed, malice, deceit, licentiousness, envy, blasphemy, arrogance, folly. All these evils come from within and they defile. (Mark 7:18-23)

If the Enemy can deceive and trick the human heart, if he can bind it with all sorts of shame, self-hatred, accusation, and condemnation, if he can warp our understanding of who God is and who we are—then we are more likely to bring forth the rotten fruits of the kingdom of darkness. In other words, we are more likely to sin and reject the mercy of God in our lives.

I have seen this pattern play itself out many times in the course of my ministry, but never so clearly as in the life of a man with whom I was praying on a regular basis. "Jack" struggled for many years with an addiction to pornography. He went to the Sacrament of Reconciliation over and over again, and although he received absolution and knew on an intellectual level that he was forgiven, Jack was absolutely convinced "in his heart" that God didn't really love and forgive him because he was so "bad." Eventually, this conviction, based on a lie about who he was, caused Jack to stop going to confession altogether. A deep-seated hopelessness took root within him. It wasn't until Jack encountered the reality of Jesus' love for him in a personal way and was able to receive a healing of his self-image that he returned to the sacraments and, through God's grace, experienced freedom from his addiction.

The Enemy's Tactics

While God created us with free will, he intends that we use that will to freely choose him. The devil is a master strategist, but he can't just use his power and cast aside the freedom to choose that we have received from our Creator. Rather, Satan prefers to work in the shadows, whispering falsehoods, casting doubt, and accusing us when we are at our weakest. To be sure, lies aren't the only weapons he uses, but they are some of the most effective in his arsenal.

The human person is an amazing creation. God has given us an intellect, a will, emotions, memory, and imagination—and with these gifts we can learn from our experiences, make sense of the world around us, and respond accordingly. Every day, we take what happens to us and process it, filtering it through a host of conclusions that we have drawn from life experiences and the formation we have received from parents, family, school, and so on. This processing is heavily influenced by what we believe about ourselves, God, and the world around us. The Enemy wants us to come to the wrong conclusions, and therefore he drops lie after lie around us knowing that we may begin to internalize some of those lies. He is patient and cunning, willing to work with the inevitable trauma that comes from living in a fallen world. For example, someone who experiences a string of breakups may begin to think that they are unlovable. The Enemy may "push into" that place of weakness through memories of past breakups—until eventually the individual starts to believe that they really are unlovable.

We may also come into agreement with a lie as a way of protecting ourselves from pain or further suffering. In other words, we internalize the lie and begin to believe that it reflects some truth about us. For example, individuals who grew up in highly dysfunctional homes and coped with judgment, manipulation, and abuse, may come to believe that they don't need love. Such a lie may cause them to make inner vows not to open their hearts to anyone. Such vows are interior decisions we make that shape how we relate to God, ourselves, and others. These inner vows can powerfully protect a person—and just as powerfully keep the love of the Father from their heart.

I made such a vow when I was a young adult. A series of very painful relationship rejections in my late teen years led to an interior decision that I would never allow myself to be hurt in that way again. That vow created a kind of wall around my emotions, and I soon found myself using and manipulating others, particularly women, so that I could experience what I wanted without any kind of vulnerability or openness on my part. It wasn't until I surrendered myself to Jesus and grew in my relationship with him that I was able to repent of that vow and break its hold on me.

Once someone opens the door to a lie and begins to believe it, they give the Enemy further influence. He will, in turn, try to take that toe hold and turn it into a foothold, and then turn that foothold into an actual stronghold. Bob Schuchts, a Catholic counselor and founder of the John Paul II Healing Center, describes this process of gradual bondage in his book *Be Healed: A Guide to Encountering the Powerful Love of Jesus in Your Life*:

Strongholds begin as beliefs, rooted in our minds and hearts. They are based on Satan's lies and deception. They often develop in response to traumatic wounds that have been left unhealed. It all takes place subtly and without fanfare: A lie is planted and believed. A temptation is acted out. A wound is incurred and left to fester. . . . Before we know it, we have been brought into spiritual slavery in a particular area of our lives ~~had~~.

This slavery often manifests itself as an inability to choose to do the right thing in the area of life that is under the influence of that stronghold. No matter how often we confess, pray, or try to discipline ourselves, we end up repeating a pattern of sin or unhealthy thinking that negatively affects our lives and the lives of others. If you are experiencing such things, if there are areas in your life which seem stuck and highly resistant to the grace of God, you might be wrestling with the presence of a stronghold.

If you think of Satan's lies as his foot soldiers, then strongholds become fortresses where these foot soldiers can rest and then march out to attack other areas of our life. If not dealt with, these strongholds eventually begin to influence how we receive, process, and respond to life experiences—including how (and if) we can receive love, forgiveness, and healing. Continuing his discussion of the power of strongholds, Bob Schuchts writes that "these strongholds create barriers in our minds and hearts, which can prevent us from receiving God's love and grace."

Once we are sufficiently bound by these lies, they can become a part of our very identity, infecting the framework of our personality, our spirituality, and our relationships. In a sense, we become those lies—or at least our false self does. The truth of our identity as sons and daughters of a loving Father cannot ever be taken from us, but we can build a false identity, constructing an image of who we are that is grounded and founded upon root lies. That image is a far cry from the beautiful child of God whose Father delights in her. What might this bondage look like? A real-life example may be in order.

Several years into my tenure as the Director of Evangelization and Faith Formation at a suburban parish in the Chicagoland area, we began to offer prayer and healing for those who were suffering. Without much advertising, people began to make their way to us. One woman, let's call her Judy, came in order to be set free from anxiety and an inability to receive God's love. She knew in theory that God loved her, but she had never experienced the reality and intimacy of that love from her heavenly Father.

One evening, before prayer, she asked me a question: "How do you know that when you die, you'll go to heaven?" I didn't have to think hard about my answer. I told her the truth—that I don't spend much time reflecting on that question. I try to focus on my relationship with Jesus and trust that he will take care of the rest. After a moment's silence, her eyes opened wide. "I think I don't trust Jesus," she declared at last.

I affirmed her for her honesty and gently started asking questions. It was clear that she was a faithful daughter of the Church, and that there was a relationship with Christ present, but two things emerged: she was convinced that God did bad things to those who drew close to him (just look at what happened to his Son); and she felt completely unworthy of being loved by God. Following the promptings of the Holy Spirit, I began to ask her a bit about her relationship with her earthly father. It turns out that her father was distant, seemingly never satisfied with anything that she did, highly critical of her, and had mood swings that would sometimes turn angry.

It was no wonder she had difficulty trusting God. In this case, it really wasn't Jesus whom she didn't trust. It was the Father. In her experience, fathers were, by definition, judgmental, cold, mercurial—not to be trusted. As our conversation progressed, the root lie, the foundational deception upon which she had constructed much of her understanding of who she was and who God was, emerged. After one particularly traumatic incident in grade school, she "knew" that her father wasn't on her side. He was against her. From an early age, that lie had compromised her ability to surrender her heart to God and receive love from anyone. Judy was afraid of God the Father, but also highly desired the Father's love (which she had not really received as a child). However, she felt that she had to be perfect to deserve any of that love, and the stress of trying to live out that perfection filled her life with anxiety.

Once the lie had been exposed, we were able to invite the Lord to come and reveal his truth in prayer. Not only did Judy receive an amazing vision of the Lord's tenderness toward her as we invited God into the memory of the traumatic grade school incident, but that memory was healed. The reality of the Father's love overcame the lie which Judy had come into agreement with—that her father wasn't on her side. She was able not only to renounce that lie, and several others that were attached to it, but she also began to receive the Father's love, in Jesus, on a deep and intimate level.

Judy's story is not unique. I have heard countless variations of it throughout my years in ministry. Our Enemy is very intelligent, but he is certainly not creative. This is the same stuff that he has been peddling since the Book of Genesis. Left unchecked and unchallenged by the revelation of the Father's love in Jesus Christ, it can have disastrous consequences for our lives. Paul acknowledges the effectiveness of this tactic in his Second Letter to the Corinthians. When talking about the men and women who have rejected Christ's invitation to relationship, he writes, "The god of this age has blinded the minds of the unbelievers, so that they may not see the light of the gospel" (2 Corinthians 4:4).

Spreading the Lies

In order to be set free from this bondage, we must come to grips with the reality that the Enemy truly does try to communicate with us and influence us. In the Gospel of John, Jesus says: "When he [Satan] tells a lie, *he speaks in character*, because he is a liar and the father of lies" (8:44, emphasis mine). Jesus gives us a clear sign regarding when Satan is lying—when his lips are moving! In other words, whenever we hear the voice of Satan, whether through natural or supernatural means, we can know with certainty that he is lying. But how is it that Satan communicates with us? How do we encounter this lying voice and negative influence in our lives?

Directly. Though fallen and separated from God, Satan and his demons still retain their power as angelic intelligences. As such they can communicate directly with anyone through thoughts and feelings. To be clear, Satan and his minions cannot read our thoughts. Fr. Bamonte, president of the International Association of Exorcists, wrote in *l'Osservatore Romano* that "Satan and the spirits at his service . . . are not omnipotent beings, they cannot perform miracles, they are not omnipresent, they cannot know our thoughts or know the future" (http://www.catholicnews. com/services/englishnews/2016/exorcist-films-should-teach-how-god-always-wins-over-evil.cfm). Many of them, however, are more intelligent than we are. They have observed us from our conception and can deduce a great many things with the scope of their intellectual powers. Therefore, they often know our weaknesses and how best to use our strengths against us. A well-placed accusation, a constant barrage of negative thoughts, a series of nightmarish or oppressive dreams—they can use all of these things to move us to a place of false belief, fear, or growing hopelessness.

Through Our Wounds. The devil does not lurk behind every tree or within every shadow. He is not the direct cause of every evil or traumatic thing that happens in the world, and we are not constantly under the barrage of his direct power. The world itself is wounded by the fall, subject to futility, natural disaster, illness, and death. Our own spiritual faculties (intellect, will, emotions, and so on) are wounded as well, and our very bodies have become a source of temptation for us because of the fall. In the course of this life, we will receive wounds that can spread dysfunction, fear, anger, addiction, and on and on. While these may not be the direct influence of Satan on our lives, they bear his mark and speak his language. Even without the Enemy's supernatural power, our experience of these wounds can lead us to believe lies about who we are.

Left unhealed and unredeemed, these wounds can become a doorway and even a stronghold for the Enemy, allowing him to bring the power of his kingdom to bear and spreading dysfunction in our lives.

Through the Wounds of Others. In healing ministry, we often say "pain that isn't transformed is transferred." In other words, when we have not sought healing—whether natural, supernatural, or both—for our wounds, we often end up reacting out of our dysfunction and pain rather than from a place of freedom and peace. When that happens we hurt, rather than heal, others. We have all been in situations, whether at work, home, or even just in the ordinary circumstances of life, where the brokenness of others has caused them to lash out at us or respond in a way that is out of proportion to the seriousness of the situation. These situations, even when prompted simply by the natural wounds of another, speak the language of the Enemy to us. And once again, the devil can push into those moments, heightening the effect of what has happened.

The Good News

The purpose of this chapter is not to provoke fear, but to make us aware of the battle we are in. Fear is a tool of the Enemy and a result of his lies. The consistent message of Jesus Christ, after his resurrection, was "Do not be afraid." Jesus knew that his obedience to the Father's will had secured victory over the power of Satan. The apostle John underscores this when he writes:

> This is how you can know the Spirit of God: every spirit that acknowledges Jesus Christ come in the flesh belongs to God, and every spirit that does not acknowledge Jesus does not belong to God. This is the spirit of the antichrist that, as you heard, is to come, but in fact is already in the world. You belong to God,

children, and you have conquered them, for the one who is in you is greater than the one who is in the world. (1 John 4:2-4)

At Baptism, God dwells in us through Jesus Christ, in the power of the Holy Spirit. The author of life—Father, Son, and Holy Spirit—has drawn us into the divine life. That life cannot be overcome by any force or any opposition. "For I am convinced," Paul writes, "that neither death, nor life, nor angels, nor principalities, nor present things, nor future things, nor powers, nor height, nor depth, nor any other creature will be able to separate us from the love of God in Christ Jesus our Lord" (Romans 8:38-39).

Christ has won the victory. To see the devil behind everything and live in fear is to buy into a lie. To dismiss the devil and believe that he isn't real or is just a symbol of evil is also a lie. To recognize your enemy, all the while knowing who you are and *whose* you are, is wisdom. In our battle against the wiles and lies of the evil one we are not defenseless. The Lord has made a way for us, and in his Church we have received weapons for our victory.

Chapter Two

Our Weapons

For, although we are in the flesh, we do not
battle according to the flesh, for the weapons of
our battle are not of flesh but are enormously
powerful, capable of destroying fortresses. We destroy
arguments and every pretension raising itself against
the knowledge of God, and take every thought
captive in obedience to Christ. (2 Corinthians 10:3-5)

As Paul makes clear in this passage from his Second Letter to the Corinthians, the war we are in isn't simply against the limitations of the fallen natural order that keep us from living as God created us to live. His words about the struggle against "principalities" and "powers" (Ephesians 6:12) that we highlighted in the last chapter find a complement here: a supernatural battle can't be won using only natural weapons. The Lord, however, provides for his people, and Paul is making sure that we understand this. Our weapons are not just natural, or of the flesh. Here, Paul uses the Greek word *sarx*, translated "flesh," which can refer to the life of the body and which has an additional, more extensive, meaning of a worldview—a way of living, thinking, and acting which leaves no room for the supernatural life, presence, and reality of God. A "fleshy" worldview raises up the pursuit of pleasure, dominance, control, accolades, and prestige as the primary goals of life. It does not tolerate the presence, power, and purpose of God and his kingdom. The way of

The Ten Biggest Lies of the Enemy—and How to Combat Them

the "flesh," therefore, is opposed to the life of the kingdom of God, where "the last will be first" (Matthew 20:16) and dying leads to eternal life (cf. Luke 9:24).

And so the weapons we have at our disposal are not merely of the flesh, but have their roots in the in the dynamic, life-changing power of God. Therefore, they contain real power to disrupt the infrastructure of the Enemy and tear down strongholds built up by his lies.

Paul also understands the battlefield. The language he uses here, that "we destroy arguments" (2 Corinthians 10:4), may lead us to believe he is talking only about a rhetorical strategy and an orthodox way of thinking. But as we have seen, the mind and heart, while containing the intellect, go beyond our reason, and shape what we think and feel, and how we act. And so the power of these weapons is not just limited to arguments, but includes every pretension, every obstacle that places itself between the truth of the Father's love for us in Jesus, and our own heart. This includes negative patterns of thought, false foundational beliefs, inner vows, and false identities.

This is not simply a psychological approach to life or a kind of self-actualization popularized in countless self-help books. It is essential, for Paul, that we "take every thought captive" in obedience to Christ (2 Corinthians 10:5). In other words, the inner reality and life of the human person must be conformed to Jesus Christ. How we think, what we do with our emotions, and how we act must be rooted in the person of Jesus.

Yet it is only in Christ, through the power of the Holy Spirit, that we have access to kingdom life and can possess "the mind of Christ" (1 Corinthians 2:16). Although we receive this mind of Christ in baptism, we must begin to intentionally live out the reality of this identity. We do not emerge from the waters of baptism already perfected. We are transformed and made new—but we must cooperate with the grace we have already received and surrender more and more of our fallen selves to this new identity in Christ. The degree to which we do that is the degree to which the perfection of Christ takes root in us.

It is possible, therefore, to possess life in the Spirit of Christ, but to live out of the *sarx,* or fleshy mind. Indeed, Paul warns the people of God: "Do not conform yourselves to this age but be transformed by the renewal of your mind" (Romans 12:2). The Enemy intends for us to be stuck in the fleshy mind, and uses lies, among other things, to keep us there. The weapons of *our* warfare, however, release the reality of God's kingdom within us, conforming us more and more to Jesus, who is both the king, and the perfect manifestation of that kingdom.

The Armor of God

In his Letter to the Ephesians, Paul urges the members of Christ's Body to "put on the armor of God, that you may be able to resist on the evil day and, having done everything, to hold your ground" (6:13). The battle against the lies and work of the Enemy is not a one-sided conflict where we are hopelessly outmatched and victims to the machinations of a dark kingdom that is beyond us. We are, in fact, "children of the light" (1 Thessalonians 5:5), beloved sons and daughters of a Father who has given us his life. Therefore, we can stand our ground against Satan when we live out of this fundamental identity.

Wearing the full armor of God means to:

> Stand fast with your loins girded in truth, clothed with righteousness as a breastplate, and your feet shod in readiness for the gospel of peace. In all circumstances, hold faith as a shield, to quench all [the] flaming arrows of the evil one. And take the helmet of salvation and the sword of the Spirit, which is the word of God. (Ephesians 6:14-17)

Paul wrote this Letter to the Ephesians when he was imprisoned in Rome and may have patterned the armor on that of Roman centurions, but he draws on the prophetic tradition of Israel for its particulars. Similar elements of the armor of God appear in the Old Testament Book of Isaiah: the belt of truth and faithfulness (11:5); the breastplate of righteousness and justice and the helmet of salvation (59:17); the sandals bearing the gospel of peace (Isaiah 52:7); and the sword of the Spirit (Isaiah 49:2). All of these elements of the armor of God reflect qualities of the God of Israel or his messiah—the deliverer.

Therefore, putting on the armor of God is not like donning traditional armor that exists external to us and must be placed upon us. For having received the very *life* of God through Jesus in baptism, we bear the qualities of this *life* within us. Wearing the armor of God means living authentically as sons and daughters of God, intentionally choosing to open ourselves to that life which we have already received in Jesus. In other words, this armor doesn't require perfection from us. It isn't the purview of the spiritually advanced or elite among us. If we have been baptized, the armor is ours. All we need to do is start to say "yes" to Jesus in our lives. The more we surrender to the life which Jesus offers us, the stronger that armor becomes—and the less vulnerable we are to the lies of the Enemy.

The Arsenal

In our battle against the lies of the devil, we are not simply on the defensive. God has given us effective weaponry to break the Enemy's hold on us. Here are some of the key components of our heavenly arsenal.

Fellowship. Life together with other believers is one of the essential gifts God gives us in our fight with the Enemy. It is based on our fellowship with God. As Paul says, "God is faithful, and by him you were called to fellowship with his Son, Jesus Christ our Lord" (1 Corinthians 1:9). To have fellowship with someone is to hold things in common—interests, passions, worldviews. But Paul is driving at something deeper than just a social or ideological connection. Another word that we use for fellowship speaks of this radically deeper dimension: communion. The New Testament uses the Greek word *koinonia* to convey this reality. *Koinonia* communion, with Christ and with his body, the Church, is not simply about sharing interests or holding the same beliefs. It is about a fundamental participation in the life of those who are bound together in this union. In other words, the fellowship that we have is a sharing in divine life and human life.

When we utilize the other weapons at our disposal, they deepen our *koinonia* with the Father, Son, and Holy Spirit, and with one another. To grow more deeply in this union means greater interior freedom from the power of the Enemy.

The Sacraments. The seven sacraments are not just rituals that we celebrate to remind us of the goodness of God. They are, in a very real sense, particular encounters with the Father's love in Jesus Christ, made possible through the power of the Holy Spirit. We receive the divine life of God in Baptism. This life is sealed within us at Confirmation. It is strengthened every time we receive the Eucharist. This life is renewed and restored in us when we receive the Sacrament of Penance or Anointing of the Sick, and it configures us for particular kinds of service in Holy Matrimony and Holy Orders.

The sacraments are not magical. They require something of us. We cannot approach them as if they were items on a to-do list that, once checked off, will take care of what we need to get to heaven. We have to approach them with open hearts—and it is here that the Enemy might choose to exert influence. Often, we need healing in some area of our heart so that we are free enough to surrender more. If you are interested in experiencing the freedom Christ has promised, make consistent efforts to receive the sacraments intentionally and on a regular basis.

The Bible (The Word of God). The Bible is more than a bunch of old stories about God and his people written down so that we can remember them. It is the living Word of God. In his Letter to Timothy, Paul identifies the importance of Scripture when he writes that "all Scripture is inspired by God and is useful for teaching, for refutation, for correction, and for training in righteousness" (2 Timothy 3:16). Righteousness here means a deepening of our right relationship with God. If we want to grow in this relationship, then we must enter into God's word. It is non-negotiable, not just because it is important to learn what Scripture has to say about God, but because in it we encounter the One who is the Word of God. The author of Hebrews describes it this way: "The word of God is living and effective, sharper than any two-edged sword, penetrating even between soul and spirit, joints and marrow, and able to discern reflections and thoughts of the heart" (Hebrews 4:12).

I remember one young mom who felt a call to follow Christ and become Catholic. As we were beginning this journey of instruction with her in our parish, she said to me that she was a "blank slate." Although she had married a Catholic man and sent her children to our school, she was not raised in any faith tradition. She wanted to follow Jesus but didn't know where to start. I suggested that she read a small part of the Gospel of Mark each day.

Two weeks later, she came back to me and said, "Something is happening." When I asked her what that might be, she told me that she and her family decided to read a portion of the Gospel of Mark each night before dinner. What began as a kind of obligation became something that the whole family looked forward to. She also said that it was changing every member of her family—including her. She reported that there were fewer disagreements and fights between members of her family, including between her and her husband. She was absolutely stunned and delighted that exposing her family to God's word was increasing love and unity among them and deepening her desire to receive Jesus in the sacraments.

Prayer. Prayer isn't simply a monologue where we pour out what's on our mind and God silently listens. Prayer is an entrance into the mystery of God's love and life— the mystery of his love for us and the mystery of the pouring out of his life for us. God's desire is that we would come to know him and know ourselves in him. Therefore, if we want to grow in freedom and cast off the lies of the Enemy, we must enter into a discipline of regular prayer and give space for God to respond to what we share and to guide us. In many ways, this discipline grows the more that we engage in it. Initially, it can be useful to come before the Lord at the same time each day. This helps us to move into a pattern of daily prayer that will enable us to open our spirit to the Lord.

Intercession and the Communion of Saints. Part of the reality of the good news of Jesus Christ is that we have been called into a communion that encompasses all those who have responded to the grace of God. We are drawn in, by baptism, to the family of God that comprises all those who have gone before us—the Church here on earth, the Church being purified in purgatory, and the saints in heaven. We are never truly alone, and those who dwell in union with God have not forgotten us. They desire what the Lord desires: our freedom and salvation. Paul would say of this communion of saints that "since we are surrounded by so great a cloud of witnesses, let us rid ourselves of every burden and sin that clings to us and persevere in running the race that lies before us" (Hebrews 12:1).

The saints who have gone before us watch over us and intercede for us. Scripture instructs us to "confess your sins to one another and pray for one another, that you may be healed. The fervent prayer of a righteous person is very powerful" (James 5:16). If this is true, then the prayer of those who have preceded us and dwell with God must be exceptionally powerful. Therefore, we should not hesitate to call upon them in our journey of freedom and healing from the lies and work of the Enemy.

Several years ago, a woman came to our parish seeking prayers for her friend who was suffering from cancer. The doctors had just discovered that the cancer had spread to her friend's bones and there was little they could do. This faithful woman wanted us to pray over her on her friend's behalf so that she would be healed. Our little prayer team did just that, and I left the next day to give a presentation for the Diocese of La Crosse in Wisconsin.

After that seminar, my hosts took me to the new (at that time) Shrine of Our Lady of Guadalupe. The shrine was beautiful and something powerful happened there for me. Along the walls of the shrine were reliquaries containing relics of particular saints. I had a deep sense of the presence and personalities of these six saints as I stopped to pray in front of each reliquary. As I paused to pray before the reliquary of St. Peregrine, the sense of this saint's personality increased so greatly that I knew, in that moment, he was reaching out in prayer, especially for the woman with cancer.

I prayed with that saint for perhaps fifteen minutes, wrapped in the presence of the Lord and his mother. Even though I had known and believed in the communion of saints for my whole life, this was the first time I had experienced the friendship, love, and care of a particular saint. After that, I got up and left the shrine. I thanked the Lord for this beautiful experience and would have just filed it in my memory as a unique consolation—if I had not returned home a few days later and bumped into the woman we prayed with before I left for my trip. When she saw me, she excitedly recounted that she had called her friend over the weekend to let her know there were folks who had prayed for her healing. The woman for whom we had prayed wouldn't let her get a word in edgewise, however. The doctors in the hospital had run more tests and discovered that there were no more signs of cancer in her bones.

While she still had cancer in other areas of her body, the lack of cancer in her bones meant the doctors could now move forward with a clinical plan of treatment.

The saints are powerful allies!

Service to the World. The call to service is found in one of the most recognizable passages in the New Testament: "For God so loved the world that he gave his only Son, so that everyone who believes in him might not perish but might have eternal life" (John 3:16). God's love for the world was so great that he gave. If we, who profess to follow him, hold his life within us and want that life to grow, how can we not give for the sake of others? This kind of giving includes acts of charity and mercy, but it also encompasses applying gospel values to issues of injustice in the world today. The more we recognize Christ in the suffering and give ourselves away to relieve that suffering, the more we release the power of the kingdom of God in our own lives as well.

Spiritual Practices. In this journey of healing and freedom, the Lord may ask us to take on particular spiritual practices—like fasting and almsgiving and other disciplines—that help us discover the root lies that keep us from receiving more of the Lord. For example, when the rich young man came to Jesus, having kept every commandment and wanting to know what else he must do to receive eternal life, Jesus responded to him by saying, "Go, sell what you have, and give to [the] poor and you will have treasure in heaven; then come, follow me" (Mark 10:21). It's not that Jesus requires each one of his disciples to live a life of complete poverty. Rather, Jesus understood that the rich young man's wealth bound him and kept him from following the Lord with his whole heart. Therefore, Jesus instructed him to sell what he had. This was a spiritual practice he needed to engage in to uproot what was keeping him from the Lord. As you begin this process of freedom and deliverance, allow your heart to be open to particular spiritual practices the Lord may be asking you to consider.

Renunciation. We have received the gift of free will from our Creator. Because of that, we possess enormous freedom to choose our reactions to life and our path in this world. Even when the will is compromised by sin, by deep deception, by malaise, or even by mental illness, this freedom is essential to who we are. When we make an intentional choice to renounce lies that have been spoken over our life by ourselves, the Enemy, or others, we stop giving them authority and power. This is even more so when we renounce these things in the name of Jesus Christ.

People who receive the Sacrament of Reconciliation sometimes don't quite believe that they are forgiven, or they don't experience the fruits of that forgiveness in their life. It isn't that the sacrament "didn't work." We know by faith and the teachings of the Church that the sacraments are efficacious. But sin has a number of components. There is the guilt associated with our sin and the Sacrament of Reconciliation deals with that. But then there are the effects of sin on ourselves and the world. Sometimes, when we find ourselves in a pattern of sin, we not only need sacramental absolution, but we also need to engage our will and renounce the lies and power associated with that sin in the name of Jesus Christ. The sacrament forgives the sin and the guilt associated with it, and the renunciation helps us to break the authority of whatever is binding the will and making it more susceptible to temptation.

I remember praying with a woman I will call Denise. Denise grew up Catholic in an unstable home. As a result, she had a strong desire to control the events, circumstances, and people in her life. This urge to control affected her personal and professional life, and it led her to get involved in the occult as a way of exerting her will on the world around her. As a result, Denise began to experience not only depression, but also some manifestations of demonic activity in her life. The forces that she had bargained with now had an invitation to be present in her life, and they began to torment her.

Soon after these manifestations began, Denise returned to the Church and confessed her involvement in witchcraft. Despite this, the occult still had a voice in her life and Denise was truly struggling. As we prayed together over several weeks, Denise was able not only to renounce her involvement in the occult, but also to experience enough inner freedom that she also renounced her desire for control. This renunciation broke the authority of the occult in her life and was an intentional act of cooperation with the grace she was receiving in the Sacrament of Reconciliation and the Eucharist. She was freed of the demonic torment and experienced healing of her emotions, memory, and will.

The power of renunciation is imbedded in our Easter liturgies, where we often make a renewal of our baptismal vows. In that liturgical format, we begin with "I renounce Satan and all his empty works." The power of renunciation in Christ extends beyond liturgical celebrations and provides a potent weapon in our battle against Satan. When we use our authority in Christ to break the power of lies in our life, we are acting in harmony with the sacramental life offered through the Church.

Keeping Our Eyes on Christ

These are just some of the ways that we can grow in intimacy with God, but they are essential to a life of freedom. And yet, it is quite possible to engage in many (or all) of these practices and still remain in bondage. What makes the difference between freedom and a lack of freedom in this journey of healing? A useful image in the Gospel of Luke can help answer that question. In Luke's gospel, an angel appears to the shepherds keeping night watch and proclaims the birth of the Savior. As proof of his words, he says: "And this will be a sign for you: you will find an infant wrapped in swaddling clothes and lying in a manger" (Luke 2:12).

To be swaddled is to be wrapped tightly in cloth. We swaddle an infant inside a snug blanket, binding their whole torso, including their arms and legs, as a way of helping them to transition from their mother's womb to the outside world. Such wrapping also helps protect babies from scratching themselves, and it reduces the need for comfort items in the crib that have been linked to sudden infant death syndrome. Swaddling, therefore, protects and nurtures the infant.

There are times in our life when we swaddle our *hearts* as a way of keeping them safe. We sometimes use coping mechanisms (such as actions, thought patterns, and denials) as a way of dealing with trauma. It is possible for these coping mechanisms to become unhealthy, or for us to develop unhealthy attachments to these mechanisms. In this way, we swaddle our wounds, protecting anything or anyone from messing with them and causing us further pain—and that includes opening them to the healing action of God's grace.

We also wrap up gifts as a way of hiding their contents. While this is completely appropriate, we have a tendency to wrap up our brokenness, too, hiding it from others and, if we are honest, from ourselves. Because the Enemy has a vested interest in protecting and hiding our woundedness, he is quite willing to help us camouflage, deny, or hide our wounds.

When this is the case—when our wounds are hidden, wrapped up, protected, or shielded—even the most faithful use of the weapons of our warfare will yield little fruit. Once the Lord begins to reveal the source of dysfunction and the root lies, however, we can intentionally use the gifts that we have been given in Christ to receive greater freedom. In these cases, we begin to bear fruit in areas where we have traditionally been bound.

So far, we have talked a great deal about Satan and his works and strategies, because it is critical to know our enemy. Yet the eyes of those who long for peace and holiness should ever be focused on the One who has delivered us—upon Jesus and the reality of his kingdom. This is Paul's advice as well: "Finally, brothers, whatever is true, whatever is honorable, whatever is just, whatever is pure, whatever is lovely, whatever is gracious, if there is any excellence and if there is anything worthy of praise, think about these things" (Philippians 4:8).

As we move forward to shed the light of God's truth on some of Satan's biggest lies, this will be our focus as well. Reading a book, even one like this one, designed to help you on your journey, is not enough to experience true, lasting freedom. That freedom only comes in Jesus through his Spirit. We invite that Spirit now to pour out grace and life and hope within us, and to reveal not only the Enemy's lies in our life, but also the intimate love of the Father present for us in Jesus Christ.

Chapter Three

Battling the Lies

*O LORD, my God, I cried out to you for help
and you healed me. (Psalm 30:3)*

Every journey has a beginning—including the journey of heal-ing. Yours did not begin when you picked up this book. The Lord has been at work within you long before that, strength-ening you and preparing you for this moment. As you take this next step, take heart in knowing that the God of truth, the One who created you for freedom, will bring this work to fruition in you if you remain with him on this journey.

I have seen this in my own life. You wouldn't know this from reading my bio, but I was born with a congenital "below elbow" amputation. Basically, I was born without a right hand. Despite coming from a loving family, with very attentive and supportive parents, the words and actions of others as I was growing up led me to believe some serious lies about myself. I hated myself, convinced that I was made "wrong" and "fright-ening" and "broken." I also hated God. My whole identity became wrapped up in these lies about myself. I was wracked with anger, unable to experience real peace, or even accept love from others. What's worse, the Enemy began to "speak into" those broken places in my life, and I began to act out of that brokenness, distancing myself further from God.

It wasn't until I connected with a number of Catholic disciples in graduate school who prayed with me and witnessed Christ's love for me, that I experienced a life-changing encounter with the Father's love in Jesus Christ through the Holy Spirit. Healing and deliverance followed, and I not only understood that the Father had created me as his beautiful son, but that his Son was with me in every moment of suffering I ever experienced in my life. The Lord didn't restore my right hand, but my whole experience of living with a disability was radically changed from that moment on. Those lies no longer held any power over me. The truth of my identity emerged in that experience of love.

Looking back now, I can see that the Lord prepared me for that moment of encounter throughout the course of my life. In the wide working of his grace, there were people speaking and demonstrating truth into my life, beginning with my parents, and also including friends, family, fellow Catholics, strangers, and even people with whom I didn't agree. There was also the voice of the Lord in Scripture, in liturgy, and in the quiet depths of my heart. The actual moment of healing was a single event in a long history of God's compassionate and loving plan for me, the culmination of his patient, saving power in my life and the next stage in an ongoing adventure that will lead into eternity.

Taking the next step in your journey of healing means listening to what the Lord reveals and paying attention to where he is leading. It is important, therefore, to ask the Lord to illuminate the underlying lies that may be wrapped around our brokenness. In a culture that goes to any length to avoid discomfort, journeying into our wounds seems counterintuitive, yet this is the rhythm of the paschal mystery which reveals that the way to eternal life and freedom is the road of the cross. Choosing not to explore the wounds and their pain only allows them greater control and power in our life. Bob Schuchts emphasizes this reality in his book *Be Healed: A Guide to Encountering the Powerful Love of Jesus in Your Life*:

> When traumas are left untended they create wounds in our souls that can eventually harm our bodies and spirits in significant ways. These wounds become part of our everyday language and reveal the effects of sin in our lives. . . . Each of these wounds is a particular taste of hell, bringing torment to our soul.

These wounds harm us on a natural, psychological level and provide opportunities for the Enemy to influence us. These are the lies we will cover in this book:

1. I am alone.

2. I can only count on myself.

3. God is not a good Father.

4. The devil is as powerful as God.

5. Following God means giving up happiness.

6. God is powerless to help me.

7. I am meant to suffer.

8. I am so broken or damaged that God does not want to save me.

9. I have to be perfect (or nearly so) to earn God's love.

10. I am insignificant.

Like a spiderweb, the web of the Enemy's lies contains a confusing array of anchor points, spirals, and lines that connect together with labyrinthine complexity. They can confuse and trap us. The distinctions between these lies, therefore, can sometimes seem subtle—though their differences are very real and become much clearer when we examine their focus.

For example, the difference between the lie *I Am Alone* and the lie *I Can Only Count on Myself* rests on where we fixate within each lie. When we are bound by the lie that *I Am Alone*, we tend to put our energy and focus on the world and the people around us who have, perhaps, abandoned us. The universe is a cold and isolated place. *No one understands me.* On the other hand, the lie *I Can Only Count on Myself* locks our attention almost exclusively on ourselves and what we must do. *I have to be in control. I can't trust anyone else.*

Using This Book

The remaining chapters will use the following format, highlighting the weapons given to us by the Lord for our freedom. Consider these as tools for the journey of healing.

Speaking the Lie. The title of each chapter will be a general version of a particular lie. However, these lies manifest themselves in different ways in different people. This section of the chapter will note particular examples of the lie and make its focus clear. Although these examples are not exhaustive, reading these particular manifestations of the lie prayerfully can help reveal whether or not your life has been bound or affected in some way by that lie.

Encountering the Truth. Ultimately, each chapter will focus on the truth of God revealed in Jesus Christ. By exploring Scripture and Tradition, we uncover the fundamental truth that each lie seeks to confuse, deny, block, or subvert. This is more than a catechetical teaching or a knowledge dump. What the Bible and the teaching of the apostles reveal is none other than the person of Jesus Christ. Combined with the rest of the chapter sections, *Encountering the Truth* should help facilitate an encounter with Jesus that leads to freedom.

Unsheathing the Sword of the Spirit. This section contains passages from God's Word designed to penetrate and cut away anything related to the lie. You might find it helpful to pray for a few minutes before reading these Scriptures and ask the Lord specifically for the grace to receive exactly the message he is trying to communicate to you at this time in your life. Then read the passage(s) slowly and prayerfully several times. Take note of any words or phrases that jump out at you. When you are finished reading the passage(s), ask the Lord to shed more light on the word(s) or phrases that jumped out at you. Ask God to reveal what a word or phrase might have to do with experiencing freedom in your life right now.

Spiritual Practice. Think of the old adage "practice makes perfect." Unlike the improvement of a skill, which requires purely human qualities of commitment and repetition, breaking free from the Enemy's lies requires that we intentionally cooperate with God's grace. This section will offer concrete ways to explore the truth and live it out in daily life. When undertaken with commitment, these practices—with God's power—can help create new patterns of thought and belief that draw us more deeply into the freedom for which we were created.

Prayer of Renunciation. This isn't a magic formula or self-help mantra. This section of the chapter will provide a sample prayer of renunciation that you can repeat to break the power of that particular lie in the name of Jesus Christ. You are encouraged to make your own, spontaneous prayer of renunciation, but the prayer I will propose is there for you to use whenever you need it. You also may find it helpful to recite this prayer whenever you are particularly conscious of the lie's power.

Invoking the Saints. Here you will find brief information about a saint whose journey reveals a victory over the specific lie we discuss in that chapter. As the Lord begins to reveal the nature of the wound or lie you are wrestling with, you can ask this saint for his or her prayers and companionship.

Chapter Four

Lie #1: I Am Alone

When I was ten years old, my parents were involved in an adult softball league that played at a park a few blocks from our house. I would often ride my bike to the park and watch them play. One Saturday, I decided to leave the park and hang out with my friend Scott, who just lived a block or so away. I let my parents know, and then headed to his house. Now, Scott always had the coolest toys, and it wasn't long before I found myself absorbed in heated games of *Pong* (yes, I'm that old) and playing with Buck Rogers action figures. Truth be told, I lost track of time, and when I realized what had happened, I hastily thanked Scott for sharing his toys with me, and then I sped back to the park. Only to find that everyone—including my parents—had left.

I was completely alone. The park, which had been so loud and full of life when I left, now seemed vast and empty. I felt that I was entirely on my own, and that feeling of abandonment, that sense of loss, is something that I remember clearly almost forty years later. That feeling, that deep-rooted aloneness, is precisely the place in which the Enemy can trap us.

Scripture warns that we should "Be sober and vigilant. Your opponent the devil is prowling around like a roaring lion looking for [someone] to devour" (1 Peter 5:8). Lions are generally the most fearsome and strongest predators in their environment. Known for stealth, speed, and power, they can quickly take down their prey. If you have ever watched a video of lions hunting, however, you know that they often stalk the weakest or slowest members of a pack of animals. As they maneuver, they cut their target off from the rest of the pack and then move in for the kill.

This is the same pattern that Satan uses. His tactics are designed to make us withdraw from our human connections, to believe that we are alone, or to think that no one could possibly understand what we are going through. The more we withdraw from our communities, the more we hide what is going on with us or within us from our families, friends, and those closest to us, the more vulnerable we become to further attacks.

Often, the circumstances of broken relationships become the entry point for this lie. In other words, our parents, friends, or spouses may have abandoned us. That abandonment isn't the lie itself. As we deal with the fallout from that experience, however, the Enemy lays down a series of lies, hoping that we will get caught in one. If this experience has happened to us multiple times, we may start believing that we don't deserve to be in relationships or that there is something wrong with us, and we may begin to draw wrong conclusions from these experiences.

Again, the lie that *I Am Alone* focuses our energy and anxiety around the experience of abandonment by—and isolation from—others. In chapter five, we will explore another lie, *I Can Only Count on Myself*, whose power causes us to focus almost entirely on ourselves.

Speaking the Lie

This lie can manifest itself in various ways, including:

- ∞ "The people I love always end up leaving me."
- ∞ "No one else loves me or wants me."

- ✍ "No one understands my pain, my history, or my life; it is better for everyone if I just go away or stay away."
- ✍ "Why bother reaching out or making friends? People are just going to leave me anyway."
- ✍ "God is too busy, too big, and too distant to notice me, listen to me, or care about me."
- ✍ "I deserve to be alone."
- ✍ "God has abandoned me."

Encountering the Truth

In a culture where virtual interaction and social media take precedence over in-person contact, where relationships (including marriages) begin and end over text messages, where we record and upload our life experiences rather than being present to the people with whom we are sharing those experiences, it is easy to feel alone. Advances in technology have closed the geographical distance between people around the world, making communication and response time almost instantaneous. Yet spiritually and emotionally we are becoming more isolated than ever. Technology has definitely exacerbated the sense of isolation many of us feel, but the reality is that technology itself is not the cause of this inner gap between people—the issue has never been about technology, but about the human heart.

In the midst of these advances, and in succumbing to their appeal, we can lose sight of something fundamental: that the human heart was created for relationship. How do we know this? Because the architect of the human heart, the One who designed, shaped, and fashioned it, is the God who is love.

That may seem like an abstraction, or a greeting card sentiment, but nothing could be more radical or more radically relevant to your life right now. Love is not solitary; it does not stand alone or at a distance. Love is present. It is ready to pour itself out. Love always seeks the other, the beloved. Nowhere is this more true than in the life of the God whose nature is love so immeasurable that it cannot be contained in a single person. The Father offers everything to the Son, even the depths of his own being. And the Son, out of love and fidelity, offers everything back to the Father. In this mutual self-giving, this Divine Exchange (which has always happened and will always happen), the Holy Spirit is eternally present—the very love between the Father and the Son personified.

This Love created all of humanity—including you and me—not out of a sense of incompleteness, but rather out of a fullness. This God gazed out from eternity, down the long track of years, and loved you into existence simply because he knows that the greatest gift he can offer any creature, and the greatest experience we as creatures could ever have, is to be loved perfectly. Cardinal Joseph Ratzinger, before he was elected pope and took the name Benedict XVI, said that relationship was the reason God created the entire universe:

> All is created from the Word and all is called to serve the Word. This means that all of Creation, in the end, is conceived of to create the place of encounter between God and his creature, a place where the history of love between God and his creature can develop. . . . The history of salvation is not a small event, on a poor planet, in the immensity of the universe. It is not a minimal thing which happens by chance on a lost planet. It is the motive for everything, the motive for creation. Everything is created so that this story can exist, the encounter between God and

his creature. (Reflection of the Holy Father Benedict XVI at the opening of the 12th Ordinary General Assembly of the Synod of Bishops, October 6, 2008)

Does this surprise you? We are embodied spirits, a union of physical materiality and a soul. We are not made like the angels, who are pure spirit. Nor are we simply fashioned like the animals, who are comprised of pure matter. We are both soul and body. Our physical existence is not an accident. The Lord created us this way—and therefore we *need* a place, a geography in which to live, and move, and have our being. God created everything—including this planet, this place—in order that we can be in relationship with the One who made us.

To this end, we are unique in all creation. "Let us make human beings in our image, after our likeness," God declares in the Book of Genesis (1:26). No other part of creation bears the image and likeness of God as humanity does.

To Know and to Be Known

This has real-world implications. If we truly are made in his image, then the reality of communion, of relationship, is written into our very being, as it is in his. Indeed, in the heart of every human person lies the hunger to know another and to be known by another, to love and to be loved. Once we encounter the truth that we are made for relationship, the Accuser will bring up a laundry list of our past failed relationships, or the absence of current relationships (especially a marital one). He will try to get us to conclude that because we have not been able to start or sustain these relationships, we are somehow less than human or unable to bear the image of God in the same way as people who are "better" than we are at relationships.

But a lie can never withstand the power of truth, and when our first parents turned away from God and ruptured the communion for which we were created, the Lord came in search of us, sending his only Son. The Word of God, who is the Second Person of the Trinity, left heaven, assumed our human nature, and became one of us. This startling reality, that God became man, is not just one facet of the story. It is the entire point of the story. When the Son of God chose to live through our human nature, he "emptied himself, taking the form of a slave," God threw in his lot with his creatures (Philippians 2:7). At the Incarnation, God made a radical statement: he would not allow anything to come between him and his beloved.

Jesus, God's only Son, became one of us, like us in all things except sin. During his life on earth he "worked with human hands, he thought with a human mind, acted by human choice and loved with a human heart" (*Gaudium et Spes,* 22). This Jesus experienced the joys and sorrows of life as you and I do. In fact, at the end of his life, he experienced heartache and betrayal, and was abandoned by most of his friends. He suffered torture and a lonely, agonizingly slow death on a cross. This would lead the author of Hebrews to conclude that "we do not have a high priest who is unable to sympathize with our weaknesses, but one who has similarly been tested in every way, yet without sin. So let us confidently approach the throne of grace to receive mercy and to find grace for timely help" (4:15-16).

In other words, God cares deeply about every detail of your life, and every suffering you have endured. Jesus, God in the flesh, understands. Nothing you experience is beyond him. This

Jesus is waiting for you to turn over those burdens to him. He has already defeated them on the cross, and he longs to lift the weight of that cross from your shoulders. In him, we *are never* alone.

In the face of life's uncertainties and burdens, and in the midst of the Enemy's lies, there is someone who has never abandoned you.

His name is Jesus and he invites you into a relationship with him.

Unsheathing the Sword of the Spirit

Freedom does not come from knowing these facts about God's desire for relationship, but from opening our hearts to the reality of that relationship. Spend time each day meditating and praying through Psalm 139 verses 1-16. Ask the Lord to reveal the times you have tried to run from him and tried to close yourself off from others. As you let the words of the psalm soak into your spirit, ask the Lord also for the grace to experience the nearness with God that the psalm declares.

You might also find the following Scripture passages helpful:

- Jeremiah 29:11–14
- Isaiah 49:15-16
- Matthew 11:28–30
- Luke 12:22–34
- John 15:9–17
- Romans 8:31–39

As you work your way prayerfully through these passages, pay attention to any memories, thoughts, or emotions that come forth in response to the promises and pronouncements that God is making about his relationship with you. In particular, discovering what causes you to react negatively may give you insight into the particular manifestation of this lie that holds sway in your life.

Spiritual Practice

As you advance on the journey of healing in relation to the lie that *I Am Alone*, take time every day—perhaps in the evening—to see if you notice times when Jesus has been pursuing you. When you had a sense that he was with you, that, in fact, you were not alone. When we look through the eyes of faith at our life, we often find that the fingerprints and footprints of God become more visible to us. For example, I remember a time not too long ago when we had several unexpected household expenses. Because I support my family largely through my ministry, I do not receive a regular paycheck. Worry about finances began to consume me, and I was seriously contemplating a return to the corporate world.

In prayer, I had a somewhat angry conversation with Jesus about this. Two days later, I opened an envelope that had come in the mail from a diocese I would be working with. Inside was a check that should have been a small initial payment to reserve a particular event date. Instead, I found myself staring at a substantial amount of money. Rather than just the initial reservation fee, this diocese had paid me for the whole event in advance. This *never* happens. As it turns out, that additional money equaled the exact amount of our unexpected household expenses. It was another example of the way that Jesus "courts" my deepening trust and lets me know that I am not alone, that he is with me.

Pausing throughout the day or at its end to see where Jesus is pursuing you will help to strengthen your relationship with God. You also will want to develop spiritual practices to help you strengthen your relationships with others. Because the instinct around the lie that *I Am Alone* paradoxically prompts us to hide, withdraw, protect, and withhold from others, embracing a spiritual practice that deliberately opens us up to others is key to growing in freedom.

Here's what I suggest. The manifestations of this lie are often rooted in real experiences of hurt and abandonment. Therefore, the spiritual practice of reflecting on those hurtful experiences *in order to begin a process of forgiveness* can bear much fruit. To enter into forgiveness is to put into practice the healing response of the Gospel to the lie that we are not made for or worthy of relationship. To facilitate this, I suggest creating a Litany of Forgiveness.

In the Catholic tradition, a litany is a series of intercessory petitions with a repeated response. It can be used both for public and private prayer. In this case, the litany should include the person you want to forgive and details about what they did. You don't have to be perfectly healed, at peace, or in a good place to make the act of forgiveness. In the Unbound method of deliverance prayer, author Neil Lozano talks about forgiving from a place of pain. Conscious of the hurt we still hold while coming before the Lord and declaring forgiveness releases healing within us and opens us up to God's grace.

Putting it all together, the litany could look something like this:

Father, I thank you for the forgiveness that you offer me in your Son, Jesus.

For the time when my father refused to come to my wedding.
Response: With your grace, I forgive him, Lord.
For the time when my spouse chose to go out with friends rather than spend time with me during our planned date night.
Response: With your grace, I forgive him, Lord.

And so on. Submitting these hurts and wounds to the Lord in this way breaks their power to act as an opening for the Enemy to push in.

Prayer of Renunciation

When you are ready, take the insights you received from the *Encountering the Truth* section and from praying through the Scripture passages, and bring them to the Lord in prayer. If you are conscious of particular memories that reinforce this lie, you can invite the Lord to reveal where he was in your life during the times those situations were happening. We often see only a part of the truth, but the Lord can reveal to us the whole of what happened and how he was walking with us during those times. You may need to repeat this renunciation prayer regularly as you make this journey of healing:

> Heavenly Father, I thank you for all that you have done for me, from the moment of my creation. Thank you for making me your beautiful child and declaring your Fatherhood over me. You know the history of my heart, Lord, and you know I can't always accept the gifts you have for me. Today, I ask for the grace to release to you those inner vows, fears, and judgments that keep me apart from you and my brothers and sisters.

In the name of Jesus Christ, and by the power of the Holy Spirit, I renounce and reject all belief that I am alone or deserve to be alone. I break now all authority and power that these false beliefs and lies have in my life, and I intentionally claim now the Fatherhood of God over myself and my family. I come against every lie planted to make me feel isolated and take authority over them in the most holy name of Jesus Christ. I thank you, Father, for welcoming me into your family, and for the freedom you offer me in your Son, Jesus. Amen.

Invoking the Saints

> *"If we have no peace, it is because we have forgotten that we belong to each other."*
> *St. Teresa of Calcutta (1910–1997)*

One of the most recognizable and popular saints of the twentieth century, St. Teresa (born Anjezë "Agnes" Gonxhe Bojaxhiu) dedicated herself to serving Christ in the poorest of the poor. In 1950 she founded the Missionaries of Charity, a religious order that, among other works of mercy, manages homes for people dying of HIV/Aids, leprosy, and tuberculosis, and runs soup kitchens, mobile clinics, orphanages, and schools. Teresa saw Christ in the "distressing disguise of the poor," and believed that no one, regardless of their poverty, should live (or die) abandoned by the human community.

Although her early life as a Sister of Loreto was characterized by several mystical experiences and encounters with Jesus Christ, her personal journals and the testimony of her spiritual directors reveal that St. Teresa experienced a searing and extended dark night of the soul—a period of over fifty years where she felt no presence of God whatsoever, whether in prayer, the sacraments, or in her missionary work. Through the working of God's grace and her cooperation with that grace (even though she could not understand her circumstance), St. Teresa faithfully lived out her vocation. We can approach St. Teresa and have confidence that she understands those who struggle with the lie that we are meant to be alone, that we are not made for relationship.

Chapter Five

Lie #2: I Can Only Count on Myself

As I have grown in age, experience, and in my relationship with Christ, it has become clearer to me that Christianity would be easy if it weren't for other people! I recognize more readily now the way the faults, foibles, and sins of others cause me to stumble. The reality is that some people in this life will disappoint and possibly even hurt us. They will drop the ball, betray, back out of agreements, live differently than they say they will, act out of their own woundedness, and otherwise choose themselves over us.

When that happens, the Enemy begins to whisper in our ears that we can only count on ourselves. When this lie is embraced, or reinforced by further experiences, a pattern of thinking can emerge that sees the world as an antagonistic or dangerous place that individuals can only navigate if they rely solely on themselves. Those who suffer from the effects of this lie in their lives often have a difficult time letting themselves become vulnerable. Their approach to relationships can become highly guarded, with very few people allowed behind personal defenses. In extreme cases, other people are primarily viewed as potential competition or even threats. Asking for help from others can seem weak or unwise and only happens with great difficulty.

People struggling with this lie often have control issues and deal with a lot of fear and anxiety in their life. The lie that *I*

Can Only Count on Myself shrinks our vision, causing us to fixate almost entirely on ourselves.

When experiences of abandonment include a sense of being abandoned by God, individuals can reject or disbelieve altogether the spiritual dimensions of life, preferring to deal only with what is real and measurable. Whether rooted in human brokenness or in a problem with God, this lie often generates defense mechanisms and coping skills geared toward protecting the heart. This protection can soon become a kind of tomb whereby the heart is buried and the person rejects the possibility of intimacy, forgiveness, love, and peace with God and other people.

Living under the influence of this lie means living out of what Paul calls "the flesh" (Romans 8:6). Again, when Paul uses this phrase, he is not passing judgment on the body. For Paul, living according to "the flesh" means living oriented toward things of this world, things that are passing. That's why he writes that "the concern of the flesh is death" (8:6). There is a distinction between what is true, holy, and eternal, and what is not. "The flesh" sees life only through the lens of this world, and not the kingdom of God. It is highly individualized, focused on the "I," and does not admit to anything beyond itself.

Again, the experience of being abandoned or betrayed is not the lie. In fact, the reality may very well be that at a certain period of time in your life you were the only one that you could count on. The trap here lies in the creation of a pattern of thinking where no one else can ever be trusted, including or especially God. This is the aim of the Enemy, to move us into this pattern so that we hold onto the reins of our life and refuse to let others in.

Speaking the Lie

This lie manifests itself in several ways:

- ∞ "I can't trust anyone because people have let me down, betrayed me, or not shown up for me."
- ∞ "The only person I am safe with is myself."
- ∞ "I have to look out for 'number 1.'"
- ∞ "You only live once."
- ∞ "Asking help from others means I'm weak."
- ∞ "I am the only one who can be trusted with the things that are important in my life."
- ∞ "I don't need anyone else in my life. I can do everything on my own."
- ∞ "If I rely on others, I'm just asking to be disappointed."
- ∞ "The world and other people are trying to get me."

Encountering the Truth

Because God is relational, we who have been baptized into that life enter in to that relationship. Entering into communion with God, however, also means entering into communion with all those who are in relationship with him. The kingdom of God is not primarily about individual salvation but about God's people united with each other in him. Living out this communion requires vulnerability, openness, a willingness to forgive, and a recognition that we need forgiveness. Life in the kingdom, therefore, is about mutuality and interdependence; it is communal, not solitary.

In fact, the truth of the communal dimensions of our life in Christ together is so powerful that Paul recognizes it as our primary identity. He writes: "Now you are Christ's body, and individually parts of it" (1 Corinthians 12:27). Our fundamental identity as a community, as a body, precedes our identity as individual members of that body. For Christians, our lives *do not make sense in isolation from one another*. The Fathers of the Second Vatican Council express it this way: "Man, who is the only creature on earth which God willed for itself, cannot fully find himself except through a sincere gift of himself" (*Gaudium et Spes*, 24).

I often use the example of a charcoal briquette to demonstrate this reality. I grew up in a house where my father refused to cook anything on a gas barbecue grill. He always said that the food tasted better when you used charcoal. So, we would wait—sometimes patiently, often not—for those charcoal briquettes to heat up. Early on, I noticed that the individual briquettes caught fire faster, burned hotter, and lasted longer when they were touching other briquettes. The outliers, the charcoal that had rolled off to the corner of the grill, either never caught fire, or burned out quickly. The same is true of baptized Christians. We are like charcoal briquettes—we burn brighter, hotter, and longer when we draw up next to one another and offer each other our light and heat.

This is not simply a theoretical reality. Living for one another should be rooted in concrete acts of love and kindness. "Bear one another's burdens," Paul instructs us, "and so you will fulfill the law of Christ" (Galatians 6:2). Just as two spouses support each other in word and deed within a healthy marriage, so our union with each other as baptized men and women should be tangible and should be expressed in the way we place each other first.

When I pray for men and women who suffer under the effects of this lie, the image of a heart being held in a closed fist often comes to mind. I recall a childhood memory—the time my mom brought home a small solar calculator. I thought this was one of the neatest things I had ever seen, and so I grabbed the calculator and closed my hand around it, wanting to protect it from all kinds of harm. The problem was, it required light to function, and my very act of protecting it cut the calculator off from what it needed to actually function.

In order for our hearts to receive the light, mercy, love, and healing that they need, we must learn to open our fists and offer what they contain to the Lord and to others. Releasing control and the need to live only for ourselves are big steps. Thankfully, we do not need to carry the burden of this lie throughout our life. Jesus himself invites us to receive release and relief. "Come to me," he says, "all you who labor and are burdened, and I will give you rest. Take my yoke upon you and learn from me, for I am meek and humble of heart; and you will find rest for yourselves. For my yoke is easy, and my burden light" (Matthew 11:28-30).

Unsheathing the Sword of the Spirit

As you journey through the healing process for this lie, take time each day to pray through the following passage of Scripture:

> If there is any encouragement in Christ, any solace in love, any participation in the Spirit, any compassion and mercy, complete my joy by being of the same mind, with the same love, united in heart, thinking one thing. Do nothing out of selfishness or out of vainglory; rather, humbly regard others as more important than yourselves, each looking out not for his own interests, but [also] everyone for those of others. (Philippians 2:1-4)

And reflect on these questions:

- What might it mean to be "of the same mind" with your brothers and sisters in Christ?
- What are three concrete things you can do this week to allow others to come first in your life?

Here are some additional Bible passages for you to use on your journey:

- Deuteronomy 31:6
- Isaiah 40:31
- Isaiah 41:10
- Romans 1:11-12

Spiritual Practice

As you intentionally combat the lie of thinking that *I Can Only Count on Myself*, spend time each day reflecting on how the Lord responds to others as revealed in Scripture. In what ways are you beginning to discover or find him as you put other people first? Recognize that God can speak and reveal himself to us in various ways, including in our hearts, through other people, in the circumstances of our daily life, in the liturgy, and in Scripture.

For those of us who struggle with wanting or needing to be in control, asking for help from others can be exceptionally difficult. During the time that you are walking this journey of healing, identify situations where you could use someone's help and then ask people to help you! Take note of what emotions or thoughts came up as you turned to them for help, as well as during the times they assisted you.

Finally, make an effort to engage in charitable activity and almsgiving. Rather than just donating money, make it an experience of human interaction, such as serving in a soup kitchen, distributing goods at a food bank, or volunteering at a shelter. After you are finished volunteering, ask the Holy Spirit to reveal any areas in you that resisted the experience. Offer that area of resistance to the Lord, possibly using the renunciation prayer below.

Prayer of Renunciation

Once you have had some time to reflect on the Scripture passages and are ready to come before the Lord in prayer, offer these (or similar) words to the Lord:

> Heavenly Father, I thank you for giving me the strength to take care of myself even when those who were supposed to care for me didn't. I want to be free of all lies that have led to a need for me to be in control or to not trust others. In the name of your Son, Jesus Christ, I renounce all judgments, inner vows, and thought patterns that reinforce the belief that I can only rely on myself. I break now, by the Blood of the Lamb, all power, influence, and authority of the wounds of abandonment, and renounce all lies that I have come into agreement with.
>
> Father, your Son said that he is "the way and the truth and the life" (John 14:6). I claim that life in his name and set aside control over my life through his grace. You know my heart, Lord, and the difficulty I have in asking for help. Open that heart so I may come to see reliance upon others as an expression of love and not weakness. Help me, Lord, to forgive those who may have

abandoned or betrayed me in any way. In your mercy, bind up their wounds and help them to become whole.

I pray all of this in the most precious and glorious name of Jesus Christ.

Invoking the Saints

"It is the measure of his love for man. Jesus wanted to take upon himself the separation between God and man and men from each other . . . and he bridged the infinite gap of that separation. Jesus the Forsaken is the key to unity— the crucified and forsaken Jesus."
Servant of God Chiara Lubich (1920–2008)

Chiara was born in Trent, Italy and hoped to study philosophy at university. She had a life-changing religious experience during World War II and gave her heart over to Christ. As she grew in her relationship with God, she had a deepening desire to help others see that we were made for communion with each other. In 1943, she founded the Focolare Movement, an organization that seeks to promote the peace and unity of all peoples in the world.

Chiara understood that Jesus embraced abandonment for our sake, and because he abandoned himself to the Father on the cross, we are called to abandon ourselves for the sake of others and to reach out in love and live for one another. Her ministry sought to manifest the Lord's desire for unity (John 17:21) in and among peoples and communities through prayer, dialogue, and service to one another. She truly lived for others. In this way, she is an exceptional companion for those who are seeking freedom from the lie that *I Can Only Count on Myself*.

Chapter Six

Lie #3: God Is Not a Good Father

In his 1965 science fiction classic, *Dune*, Frank Herbert created a quasi-religious organization bent on controlling the galaxy through various means of manipulation.

This group embraced a syncretic mixture of Eastern philosophical practice, Machiavellian tactics, and eugenics programs to become a major force in the galaxy. Part of their work involved mind/body meditation, and they created a Litany Against Fear which begins with the phrase *I must not fear; fear is the mind-killer*. While Herbert most likely did not have Christian anthropology at the forefront of his thinking while writing that book, he nevertheless uncovered something important: Fear is a powerfully destructive force in the heart and mind of humanity.

More than a clever science fiction plot device, fear is a major doorway for the Enemy to bully, harass, and cow us. Fear keeps us from embracing our authentic identity as sons and daughters of God who were created with real dignity. It often causes us to act out against each other, against God, and, therefore, against our own good. There is an adage in the corporate world that goes: "If you want to discover the source of corruption, follow the money." A similar one exists in the spiritual life: "If you want to discover the source of certain wounds, follow the fear."

Fear is not of God. In fact, the apostle John, in writing about the reality of God's nature as love, informs us that "There is no fear in love, but perfect love drives out fear because fear has to do with punishment, and so one who fears is not yet perfect in love" (1 John 4:18). When we rest at the center of God's love for us, we will not fear.

This is why the Enemy often attempts to move us into a place of fear. One of his classic tactics—in fact, the very first one that we see him employ in Scripture—is to try to convince us that our heavenly Father is not a good father. If, through the Enemy's lies and manipulation, we start seeing God as opposed to us, or even indifferent to what we go through in this life, then we are far more likely to experience fear—of God, other people, and even life itself.

My experience with the ocean offers an example of the effect of fear once it has been embraced. I grew up in a suburb of Long Island, not too far from the Atlantic Ocean. During the summers, my family would visit Jones Beach. When I was younger, I spent all my time in the water, swimming across the cresting waves and allowing them to carry me, sometimes tumultuously, back to the shore. I loved the ocean's power, and I found it both mysterious and amazingly beautiful. For years, I didn't think twice about leaping into its expanse. For me, the ocean was more than a place; it was a friend and companion.

One day, though, during an exceptionally hot stretch of summer weather, I jumped into the water and a jellyfish stung me. The jellyfish venom really did hurt, but I experienced greater trauma from the realization that the ocean, which I had viewed almost as a playmate, could be quite a dangerous place. It didn't like me or even care about me. From that moment, I began to fear the ocean and what it hid beneath its surface—and for nearly twenty years afterward I avoided going to the beach or swimming in the ocean.

Similarly, if we believe that God is against us, or doesn't even care about us, the fear which we may experience can lead us to reject, run away from, or refuse to believe in God.

In addition, once we move to a worldview where the Father isn't a good father, we can become our own god, judging God's word and work through our own eyes. For example, a father who would cause his children to suffer is a monster, and I would certainly not give my heart to a monster. In fact, I should oppose that monster with all that I have. Likewise, a father who seemingly refuses to do anything about the death of his children certainly doesn't deserve my praise, worship, or loyalty.

In many ways, the lie about our Father's goodness acts as a doorway, making us more susceptible to the other major lies of the Enemy. People under the influence of this lie can struggle with numerous issues: anger at God and the suffering so endemic to the human condition; depression and anxiety rooted in the meaninglessness of life; fear that God may somehow do something bad to them or vent his anger upon them; and even hopelessness and despair. People who struggle with this lie that the Father is not good typically have a difficult time approaching God as a Father in prayer, and may avoid relationship with him—even though they may not have a similar issue with Jesus. However, the power of this lie and the corresponding patterns of thinking that it generates act as very powerful obstacles to experiencing and receiving God's love, mercy, forgiveness, and healing.

The Enemy's lies can also be "propped up" and nurtured by our life experiences. Some of us may have grown up in broken or unstable homes, where one or both parents were abusive. Our experience with our earthly parents and their brokenness can impact our understanding and experience of God the Father. As always, it isn't our actual experience that is the lie. Our earthly fathers and mothers may, in fact, not be good parents. The lie develops from what we conclude from these experiences and the patterns of thinking that emerge from them.

Speaking the Lie

This lie manifests itself in several ways:

- ∞ "God causes suffering and therefore is not a good and loving Father."
- ∞ "I am afraid of what God will do to me."
- ∞ "God doesn't care about the pain I'm going through."
- ∞ "If God is in control and allows me to suffer anyway, then he cares more about his own glory than he does about me."
- ∞ "God is against me."
- ∞ "God is punishing me."

Encountering the Truth

To uncover the truth behind this lie, let's return to the beginning, to the Book of Genesis. God created humanity in his image and likeness, and breathed his divine life into our first parents, Adam and Eve. In the creation story, God places them in a land of perfection, the Garden of Eden. He tells them that everything in the garden is theirs, but leaves them with one prohibition: "You are free to eat from any of the trees of the garden except the tree of knowledge of good and evil. From that tree you shall not eat; when you eat from it you shall die" (Genesis 2:16-17).

Now, we have to be very careful as we enter into this story. The Bible is a collection of books written under the inspiration of the Holy Spirit by different authors, at different times, and using different styles and genres. So, when we read Scripture, we must pay particular attention to the type of genre or literary style the author used. Genesis is a kind of mythic story. Now, to our modern ears, the word *mythic* sounds a lot like *made up* and *untrue*. However, the reality is that mythic literature uses particular metaphorical and literary forms to convey truth. It is not meant to be read in a literal fashion.

Why is this important?

If we read the beginning of the second chapter of Genesis literally, then it becomes quite easy to conclude that the Father is setting a trap for his children by offering them everything—except one particular tree. This is not the case, however, as a story from my own life helps make clear.

One day when my daughter Siena was about three and a half years old, I told her I had to go to the kitchen to make her lunch. Since she was a very active toddler, I instructed her to stay where she was, playing with the toys and videos that were in the room. Then I pointed to my desk and told her that she shouldn't, under any circumstances, eat the bag of M&Ms sitting there.

Chalk this up to my inexperience, but you more seasoned parents can see my mistake there. I drew my daughter's attention to the one thing that she couldn't have. I shouldn't have been surprised, then, when I heard the rustling of paper and the crunching of candy soon after. Looking at this from the outside, however, an observer could deduce that I was testing my daughter with a temptation that she would very likely find irresistible.

Reading the second chapter of Genesis in a literal sense could lead us to a similar conclusion: The Father was baiting a trap for his children, knowing they couldn't resist. What father, if truly good, would do such a thing? But if we look at Genesis more broadly, in the context of its literary style, we can see that the prohibition against eating the fruit of the tree of the knowledge of good and evil represents the limitations of Adam and Eve as creatures. In other words, they were not gods; they were not the beginning and end of their own destiny. Our first parents were created beings with limitations—unlike the Lord, who is uncreated, eternal, and all powerful.

Along comes Satan, the one opposed to the work and will of God. He enters the garden and immediately begins his deceiving agenda. Knowing full well the prohibition the Lord set for his children, the serpent asks Eve if she can eat anything in the garden. When she replies and repeats the Lord's command not to eat of the fruit of the tree of the knowledge of good and evil "or else they will die," the Enemy utters the first lie in Scripture: "You certainly will not die! God knows well that when you eat of it your eyes will be opened and you will be like gods, who know good and evil" (Genesis 3:4-5).

There it is. The insinuation that the Father is somehow lying to Adam and Eve, and that he does not have their best interests at heart. As we read further, we learn that Eve now looks on the tree and sees all the positive things that would come from the experience of eating its fruit. The Enemy's lie has taken hold of her, and we watch as the trust she had in the goodness of God, her Father, breaks apart. She eats the forbidden fruit and gives it to Adam, who also eats of it.

We see what the lie of the Enemy has done. Adam and Eve, in eating the fruit, choose not to accept their nature as created beings and the role of the Father in their life. They choose to reject the fatherhood of God and to become gods over their own lives. In a very real sense, they reject their dependence upon God and separate themselves from his life. In doing so, they make a kingdom of their own will. Ironically, in choosing to be free of God, they make themselves slaves to sin and citizens of the kingdom of darkness.

Now everything falls apart. Disease, natural disasters, death, sin, and suffering enter the world—not as a punishment from a petty God who is angry at his children's decision, but as the consequence of our first parents' intentional rejection of the divine life that they received from God. Though expressing this truth using figurative language, the Bible reveals that God is not the author of suffering, illness, and death. They do not originate with him, but rather, in the lies of Satan and the choice of humanity to believe those lies and walk away from God. This is why Jesus calls Satan a "murderer from the beginning" (John 8:44). He knows that behind the fall of humanity, behind the evil of sin, illness, death, and suffering, lurks the shadowy and real figure of Satan.

So, if God isn't the author of suffering, if evil, death, and illness really come from Satan and the choice to turn away from God, then why do bad things happen to good people? If God is really a good Father, how could he let this happen?

That is a very good question, and one that is at the heart of the mystery of suffering in this life. The reality is that God, being all powerful, could very easily snap his fingers and reverse the effects of the fall. He could have easily started over with Eden

2.0. If he had done that, we wouldn't have to deal with suffering at all in this world.

But if God exercised his power and reversed the effects of the fall, he would trample on, overpower, and nullify our free will, given to us as creatures made in his image and likeness. Love cannot be coerced, and so God leaves us free to choose to love or to reject love. Out of love for us, and a desire to give us the freedom to truly choose love, he allows the effects of the fall to play out.

But the story doesn't end there. In his love for us, the Father doesn't leave us sitting in all that suffering. He does something remarkable. God is not silent and withdrawn in the face of human suffering. He has spoken a single word, The Word, into the midst of the tragedy, brokenness, and pathos of the human condition. And as Scripture attests, this Word has power to change things:

> Yet just as from the heavens
> the rain and snow come down
> And do not return there
> till they have watered the earth,
> making it fertile and fruitful,
> Giving seed to the one who sows
> and bread to the one who eats,
>
> So shall my word be
> that goes forth from my mouth;
> It shall not return to me empty,
> but shall do what pleases me,
> achieving the end for which I sent it. (Isaiah 55:10-11)

The Father comes after us, sending his Son to enter human suffering and transform it from the inside. United to Jesus, our suffering is no longer meaningless and endless. There is a way through our suffering, a way that leads to life, wholeness, healing, and integrity. In my own life I can say, God did not give me a disability. Growing up without a hand was not in the perfect will of the Father. It was the consequence of being born into a fallen world. And yet, every moment of difficulty—and every moment of suffering that stems from this disability—is an opportunity to turn to the goodness of the Father in Jesus Christ.

The Father *is* a good father. He has not abandoned us to suffering and death. In his Son, Jesus, the power of death has been broken and our whole experience of suffering is transformed.

How would your approach to life, relationships, and prayer change if you lived from the foundational belief that God is a good Father who wants our happiness and ultimate fulfilment? This is the invitation the Lord extends to you!

Unsheathing the Sword of the Spirit

As you journey through this process of healing, spend time each day with Scripture. You may want to use all of the following verses or you may want to choose one, reading it slowly and circling any words or phrases that catch your attention. Again, take note of what thoughts, images, memories, or emotions emerge during this time with the Word of God.

- 2 Chronicles 30:9
- Psalm 100
- Matthew 7:11
- Ephesians 1:3-5

- Philippians 4:6-7
- James 1:16-18

Spiritual Practice

The story of salvation is, ultimately, the story of the Father's great love for us made manifest in his Son, Jesus Christ. The Father does not want us to be overwhelmed by the power of sin and death, nor does he desire our suffering. Like the father in Jesus' parable of the prodigal son (see Luke 15:11-32), who catches sight of his child from a long way off because he is deliberately looking for him, God the Father seeks after each of us. He has sent his own Son, Jesus, to bring us back. This Jesus comes into conflict with the powers of brokenness, sin, and suffering and emerges triumphantly from the grave, filled with the resurrected life of God's kingdom.

Think about your own life. If you are struggling with the lie that the Father is not a good Father, bring to mind your experiences with your own father or with father figures in your life. Are those experiences somehow blocking your relationship with God the Father? In what ways? Write those experiences down and bring them to the Lord, asking for insight and understanding. If you need counseling in order to work through your pain, resolve now to get the appropriate professional help.

If you find that you have generalized resistance to authority figures in your life, take some time to reflect on why that is so and how Jesus can help you work through that conflict. Specifically invite the love of the Father into those places of conflict in prayer each day.

In addition, take some time during the week to make a list of the positive aspects of your life. Where are you seeing healing, growth, fulfillment, and joy? What relationships are bringing you life? Be sure to thank the Father specifically for these experiences and areas of blessing.

Prayer of Renunciation

Once you have had some time to reflect on the Scripture passages and are ready to come to the Father in prayer, offer these (or similar) words to him:

> Father, I praise you today, not for what you have done for me, but simply for your goodness and holiness—for who you are! Help me to see more clearly the work of your goodness in my life, especially in those places of hurt, brokenness, grief, and disappointment. I renounce and reject every lie that has led me to doubt your goodness, Father, in the name of Jesus Christ, and by the power of his cross. I declare null and void any inner vows, judgments, or patterns of thinking rooted in the belief that you are not a good Father. I offer to you this day any anger, bitterness, or resentment [be as specific as possible here] that I have aimed toward you in my life.
>
> Thank you, Father, for the freedom toward which you are leading me. Open my heart so that I may live this freedom out more fully each day. I ask this in the name of Jesus Christ. Amen.

Invoking the Saints

Blessed Margaret of Castello (1287–1320) was born in Metola, Italy with severe disabilities—blind, hunchbacked, and suffering from dwarfism. Her parents were wealthy nobles who had originally wanted a son and were horrified by their crippled daughter. They kept her hidden away from others for most of her young life. When she was sixteen, Margaret's parents took her to a shrine in Città di Castello, Italy, hoping that she would be miraculously cured. When that didn't happen, they abandoned her in the streets of the city, where she had to beg to survive.

Despite her difficult life, Margaret joyfully served the poor, the sick, and those who were imprisoned. Rather than being weighed down by anger or bitterness at the circumstances of her birth, Margaret was able to forgive her parents secure in the knowledge of the goodness and love of God. She eventually joined the Dominican Tertiaries. Her cheerfulness and love of God endeared her to the poor of Castello, who would take her into their homes and support her for as long as they could, and then another poor family would take her in. Margaret died in 1320 at the age of thirty-three. More than 200 miracles have been credited to her intercession since her death. She was beatified in 1609.

Blessed Margaret knew well the realities of living in a world marred by sin and suffering. Her radical trust in the goodness of God the Father makes her a perfect companion on the journey to freedom from the lie that God the Father is a vengeful or disinterested father.

Chapter Seven

Lie #4: The Devil Is as Powerful as God

The devil possesses power—that much is certain. God created the angels as pure spirits, with intelligence and other gifts that allow them influence and power within the created order. Satan and his rebellious angels (the demons) retained these gifts even after they made their permanent choice to separate themselves from God. To deny that the Enemy has power is to blind ourselves to the reality of his ongoing work in the seduction and corruption of humanity and creation.

However, we can fall into an equally false way of thinking—one that attributes way more power to the devil than he actually has. The Enemy is an equal opportunity troublemaker. Extreme ways of looking at him—as powerless and, perhaps, metaphorical, or as real and godlike in his ability—suit him just fine. That being said, the lie that he is as powerful or almost as powerful as God is particularly potent because it can keep us from resisting his action in our life and the lives of those we love. Why bother putting up a fight? In extreme cases, the lie that Satan is all-powerful can lead us to seek influence or success directly from him.

In an age that has become increasingly distant from the reality of God's power, yet is intimately familiar with violence, terrorism, and various forms of evil, it's easy to overemphasize the Enemy's power. We see this in some of today's myths as found in books, movies, and games. Whenever evil shows up in these media, we often see the agents of an opposing power—and God, the Church, priests, and so forth—having little ability to drive back the forces of darkness.

Take, for example, the classic expression of evil's power in the movie *The Exorcist*. The demon tormenting Regan in the movie resists all attempts at exorcism, leading to the death of the experienced exorcist, Fr. Merrin (Max Von Sydow's character). The younger priest, psychologist Fr. Karras, continues the work but is frustrated by the power of the demon. Desperate to free Regan and save her from the demon's power, Fr. Karras is forced to invite the demon into him. Before the now-possessed priest can kill the young girl, he throws himself out a window, killing himself and releasing the demon. While this is, ostensibly, a demonstration of self-sacrifice, when we consider it more closely we see the power of God largely unable to do anything about the presence of evil. Fr. Karras ultimately resists the devil through purely human will. God has little to do with it.

We are surrounded by these popular stories of the Enemy's power and have absorbed their messages into our own worldview. As a result, many Catholics, including priests, are afraid to talk about Satan's work against us. Such fear causes us to avoid thinking about the Enemy and certainly deters us from standing firm against him. We don't call upon the power of God to deal with the Enemy and so remain subject to his work in our life. Knowing full well the consequences of giving in to this lie, St. Teresa of Avila famously said, "I am more afraid of those who are terrified of the devil than I am of the devil himself."

This lie can also manifest itself anytime we give someone or something else equal or greater authority than God in our life. In biblical times this was called worshiping idols. Idols don't have to be negative things. Positive, life-affirming things such as family, work, and even ministry can become idols anytime we consistently place them before God. When we idolize something, we begin to shape our thinking, actions, and lifestyle around that thing or person, and we become fearful that we might lose it.

Speaking the Lie

This lie manifests itself in several ways:

- ∞ "I should basically hide from the devil and not attract his attention, or else I'll be in trouble."
- ∞ "I don't want to talk about the devil or even think about his activity. He is too powerful."
- ∞ "I'm going to lose any battle with the devil, so I shouldn't even resist."
- ∞ "If God won't protect me [or give me success or control], maybe the devil will."
- ∞ "God is important, but I have to focus on this thing [or action or person] because they are more real."
- ∞ "I don't have to pray or give time to God; my life is my prayer."

Encountering the Truth

The devil may have power, but it cannot compare to the power of God. Our susceptibility to the lie that Satan is all-powerful stems in part from our misunderstanding of who God is. The Lord is not the most powerful being in the universe, a kind of super-being among other beings. He is entirely Other, outside of created reality entirely. Another way to express this is to say that God is Being itself, and the life of every being in the universe comes from him. Sometimes we can end up thinking that if God's power is a ten, then Satan's must be a nine, and that in any conflict between them, the outcome is unsure.

Even in the first moments of his rebellion, when Lucifer, one of the most powerful of the angels, rejected God and convinced other angels to follow him, we see the overwhelming power of God on display:

> Then war broke out in heaven; Michael and his angels battled against the dragon. The dragon and its angels fought back, but they did not prevail and there was no longer any place for them in heaven. The huge dragon, the ancient serpent, who is called the Devil and Satan, who deceived the whole world, was thrown down to earth, and its angels were thrown down with it. (Revelation 12:7-9)

This triumph of God's power is told also in the Book of Isaiah. Although in a literal sense this is a prophecy of the fall of the king of Babylon, Scripture functions on multiple levels. The Church Fathers saw this as a clear proclamation of the fall of Satan and his legion of angels.

> How you have fallen from the heavens,
> O Morning Star, son of the dawn!
> How you have been cut down to the earth,
> you who conquered nations!

In your heart you said:
"I will scale the heavens;
Above the stars of God
I will set up my throne;
I will take my seat on the Mount of Assembly,
on the heights of Zaphon.

I will ascend above the tops of the clouds;
I will be like the Most High!"

No! Down to Sheol you will be brought
to the depths of the pit! (Isaiah 14:12-15)

Vanquished by the power of God and cast out of heaven, the Enemy set himself against the will of God in pursuit of the crown of God's creation, humanity. Through his lies and prompting, humanity turned against God. Because we can trace the reality of evil, suffering, and sin to the work of Satan, Tradition refers to him as the prince of this world. Yet it was precisely to vanquish the power of sin, death, suffering, and evil that the Lord sent his only Son to become one of us. Through the life, death, resurrection, and ascension of Jesus, the power of the kingdom of God overcame the power and influence of the prince of this world. "Indeed," the apostle John writes, "the Son of God was revealed to destroy the works of the devil" (1 John 3:8).

Far from being as powerful as God, the devil has already lost!

The victory belongs to Jesus Christ and his kingdom, and the Lord released the power of this kingdom at Pentecost when the Holy Spirit came upon the disciples in the upper room and constituted the Church. Each and every member of this Body of

Christ receives at baptism the same Spirit that fell upon the disciples, and therefore the authority and power of that kingdom.

If we remain close to Christ, fruitfully participate in the sacramental life of the Church, and invite the truth of God into our lives, we have little to fear, even from extraordinary manifestations of the Enemy's power. "Resist the devil," James exhorts the Church, "and he will flee from you" (James 4:7). Our Father is all-powerful, and he has given his children a share in his power and freedom. Rather than fearing the Enemy, we should stand up secure in our identity as beloved sons and daughters, so that we can see in our own lives what Jesus spoke of when his disciples returned from their mission to teach, preach, and heal in his name: "I have observed Satan fall like lightning from the sky. Behold, I have given you the power 'to tread upon serpents' and scorpions and upon the full force of the enemy and nothing will harm you" (Luke 10:18-19).

One day several years ago, I had a parishioner come to me greatly troubled. She told me that for about a week she was having nightmarish and unsettling dreams that not only woke her up, but also made it impossible for her to go back to sleep. The sleep deprivation and growing sense of fear were taking their toll. After a few more minutes of talking, this parishioner leaned in and whispered to me that she felt as if the devil was harassing her.

Though I never dismiss these kinds of things out of hand, I also don't believe the devil is around every corner. This woman and I spent some time in prayer and discernment, after which it was clear, based on some things she told me, that the Enemy was up to something. I instructed her to receive the Sacrament of Reconciliation and come back to me for prayer—which she did. As we started to pray, I simply led her in a renewal of her baptismal promises and asked her to make a declaration of her freedom as daughter of God in the name of Jesus.

That was all it took. Her dreams returned to normal and she was able to experience peaceful and recuperative sleep. The Enemy had fled. This is the power of God which is poured out for us!

Unleashing the Sword of the Spirit

Spend time with the following Scripture passages as you walk through the process of healing from this lie:

- Isaiah 42:13
- John 12:27-36
- John 16:32-33
- Revelation 12:10-11
- Revelation 17:14

Spiritual Practice

Making something into an idol in our life can be a gradual process. During this time of focused attention on the healing journey, make a list of all the priorities in your life and begin to reflect on where these priorities fall in relation to God. Imagine that the Lord asked you to stop participating in activities that you have given priority to. How would you respond? What feelings, memories, or thoughts come to mind? This process can help you discover what you might have, unwittingly, raised up as idols in your life. If you can, give these idols over to the Lord. Imagine yourself pulling these idols out of your heart and raising your hand up to God so that he can take them from you.

If you have participated in any occult or new age practices in your life, and you have not confessed this in the Sacrament of Reconciliation, do so as soon as possible. This includes participating in such things as witchcraft, séances, tarot card readings, use of a Ouija board, astrology, reiki, palm readings, and so forth. Then include those specific practices in the prayer of renunciation below.

Prayer of Renunciation

Once you have had some time to reflect on Scripture and are ready to come before God in prayer, offer these (or similar) words to the Lord based upon your own history and life experience:

> Praise be to you Father, Son, and Holy Spirit, who alone are glory, and power, and majesty. I thank you, Lord, that in your pure goodness you have not forgotten me but offer to me your divine life in Jesus Christ. Uproot in me, by the work of your Spirit, all strongholds built on the fear of Satan, and help me cast down any idols I have made in place of the worship and relationship that you alone deserve.
>
> I reject the Enemy's works and lies, and in the name of Jesus I renounce any invitation I might have given to the kingdom of darkness to work in my life. I repent of any participation in occult works, freemasonry, witchcraft, astrology, and all practices that have their roots in Satan's domain.
>
> Today, I claim the freedom of God's kingdom and release that freedom into my life and the life of my entire

family. Give me the grace, Lord, to open myself more and more to your Holy Spirit as I grow in intimacy with you. I thank you for the peace, freedom, and joy that come from your Son's Sacred Heart. I ask all of this in Jesus' name. Amen.

Invoking the Saints

The title *saint* comes from the Latin word for "holy." All of God's angels who chose to remain with him are holy, and the Church has a special reverence for the three archangels mentioned in Scripture—Raphael, Gabriel, and Michael. When Satan rebelled against God because he refused to serve and wanted to be like God himself, Michael led the heavenly host to drive Satan out of heaven. Michael's name, which means "Who is like God?" is a kind of battle cry, a repudiation of the tendency that we have as fallen creatures to either want to be the god of our own lives or want to raise something up in our lives in place of God.

He is steadfast and ready to come to our aid as we journey toward freedom in Christ Jesus. Pope Leo XIII created a prayer to St. Michael, and this prayer is particularly appropriate to use in your journey toward freedom:

St. Michael the Archangel, defend us in battle. Be our defense against the wickedness and snares of the Devil. May God rebuke him, we humbly pray, and do you, O Prince of the heavenly hosts, by the power of God, cast into hell Satan, and all the evil spirits, who prowl about the world seeking the ruin of souls. Amen.

Chapter Eight

Lie #5: Following God Means Giving Up Happiness

Have you ever noticed that some Christians act as if they have been baptized in pickle juice? Rather than exuding the joy of following Jesus, they radiate perpetual sourness, and dampen whatever excitement and hope might be present in a meeting or gathering. The message they telegraph is that following Christ is a burden that places a heavy weight on us. They emphasize the rigors of obligation in the Christian life and sometimes act surprised when talk of joy, fulfillment, or happiness enters into the conversation. In a discussion with one such person regarding the challenge of attending Mass on Holy Days—especially when those days fall close to a Sunday obligation—his response was "Well, it's supposed to be hard!"

When I was young, I thought that this dour attitude was the default position of Catholicism—that to follow Christ, I would have to resign myself to a life of constant sackcloth and ashes. This was a natural outcome of the type of religious formation I was receiving as a preteen and teen—an overwhelming dose of the Church's moral teaching with little reference to the One from whom that teaching flowed. Catholicism, therefore, consisted of a laundry list of "thou shalt nots" rather than the adventure of following Christ in the midst of the world. Why would I give my life away to something that would make it two-dimensional and lacking in essential flavor? I wrestled with that question for a long time.

Behind this question, though, is a subtle kind of fear—and the Enemy will try to magnify it, drawing that fear out with a trail of lies. Pope Benedict, during the Mass inaugurating his ministry as pope, identifies this fear clearly:

> Are we not, perhaps, all afraid in some way? If we let Christ enter fully into our lives, if we open ourselves totally to him, are we not afraid that he might take something away from us? Are we not, perhaps, afraid to give up something significant, something unique, something that makes life so beautiful? Do we not then risk ending up diminished and deprived of our freedom? (April 24, 2005)

This is precisely Satan's tactic, to once again move us into this place of fear. Bound by the belief that following Christ will diminish our life, we will hesitate to commit ourselves to him, hesitate to lay our destiny in his hands. Once we are in a place of hesitation, the Enemy has more opportunities to surround us with his lies.

I experienced a version of this fear in my own life. The truth is, I'm a major nerd. Not only am I an avid science fiction and fantasy fan, but I also love playing computer games. Growing up, my friend James and I would spend countless hours in front of his Atari 800 game system. I retained this love of game playing into adulthood. As a vice president for a subsidiary of Hasbro, I actually took vacation days when a new game would "drop." I'd finish up my workday on a Thursday, head to the store, pick up the computer game (this was before you could download everything from the cloud), as well as a ton of unhealthy snacks, and then go home. Once at home, I would change into pajamas and then proceed to play computer games for sixteen or more hours a day until Monday morning when I would finally shower and drive back to work.

This was my regular way of relaxing, but during this time I ended up meeting the woman who would become my wife. Although I knew pretty quickly that I was in love, and that the Lord was calling us to marriage, there was a very strong part of me that hesitated in making a commitment. I had a strong suspicion that if we were to get married, I probably wouldn't be able to play computer games as much as I wanted. I recognize how ridiculous this sounds, but for me at that time in my life, the fear of losing something that I deeply enjoyed, that gave life flavor, led me to hold back on making a commitment.

The Enemy is smart. He knows that not everyone will be susceptible to the lie that following Jesus will bring great and terrible suffering. Therefore, he lays down a lie that sounds much more plausible—that following Jesus will strip us of simple joys and any human happiness. If we give this lie power in our lives, we will resist giving the Lord control in our lives. We will find ourselves mired in anxiety that is rooted in the fear that God plans on taking something from us. When we start to see God as a kind of competitor to our happiness, we are viewing the world through Satan's lens. This makes us, in turn, far more susceptible to the other lies in his arsenal.

Speaking the Lie

There are numerous ways that this lie manifests itself in our lives:

- ✎ "If I let God in, I will never be happy."
- ✎ "God cares about his laws more than my happiness."
- ✎ "Following Christ is about being miserable."
- ✎ "Christianity is boring and has nothing to offer me."
- ✎ "Holiness is dreary and unexciting, not something I would be interested in."
- ✎ "I'll live my life and have my fun now, and follow him later, when I have done the things that I want."

Encountering the Truth

The way of Christ is the way of the cross—the way of surrender and self-giving. We must never lose sight of that. A Christianity that avoids the cross is not authentic. A Christianity that avoids joy, however, is equally inauthentic. Joy is an essential characteristic of the kingdom of God (see Romans 14:17), without which the kingdom cannot be complete. This lie—that Christianity is opposed to happiness—sets a false choice before us: Either live a life of happiness and freedom or do the "right" thing—follow Christ and be constrained and miserable. Behind this worldview are two powerful concepts: fear of diminishment and lack of trust.

In contemporary society, we define freedom as the power to do whatever we want whenever we want. Our understanding of freedom has given way to a belief in unrestrained license. But the truth of human freedom, which is revealed fully in the person of Jesus Christ, is altogether different. As Pope St. John Paul II proclaimed, "Freedom consists not in doing what we like, but in having the right to do what we ought" (Homily during the Apostolic journey to the United States, 7, October 8, 1995).

To modern ears, the word "ought" connotes a tyrannical mindset bent on limiting our choices. Because the concept of "ought" flows from the presence of truth, postmodern people view truth, which is to say God, as antithetical to human freedom. God, therefore, competes with his creatures by his very existence.

And yet a quick philosophical examination of God reveals something quite different. St. Anselm, a Benedictine abbot and one of the greatest Western philosophers of the Middle Ages, would define God as that "than which nothing greater can be conceived" (*Proslogion*). Don't be thrown off by the jargon. What St. Anselm meant was simply that in order for God to be God he must be perfect and infinite, lacking absolutely nothing that is good. If he wasn't perfect and infinite, he wouldn't, by logical definition, be God. He requires nothing from his creatures, and gains nothing when we surrender ourselves to him. In fact, the more we enter into the mystery of God, the more we discover our true identity, and the more that identity becomes reality.

Becoming who we were truly created to be is an experience of the deepest freedom imaginable and brings with it fulfillment, peace, and joy. In one of Jesus' discourses, he urges his disciples to remain in his love, to remain in communion of life with him. He shares this with them "so that my joy may be in you and your joy may be complete" (John 15:11).

The fruit of our surrender is a breaking through of the kingdom of God in our lives, a manifestation of "love, joy, peace, patience, kindness, generosity, faithfulness, gentleness, self-control" beyond anything we may have experienced as we held on to those things which we were loathe to give to Jesus (Galatians 5:22-23).

Remember my hesitation in proposing to my girlfriend because I was afraid I'd have to give up playing video games? Once I actually bit the bullet and proposed, all of my fear immediately vanished. And after we were married, I discovered that my wife actually loved to play video games, too. Sure, we didn't have the opportunity for sixteen-hour marathons—especially after the birth of our daughter—but I discovered that my pleasure at playing video games was increased exponentially because my wife and I shared those experiences together.

God cannot be outdone in his desire for our happiness!

Unsheathing the Sword of the Spirit

As you walk the road of healing from this lie that God wants to deprive you of happiness, spend time meditating on the following passage from the Gospel of John. Pay particular attention to the imagery of childbirth that Jesus uses in these verses as he speaks to his disciples.

> Jesus . . . said to them, "Are you discussing with one another what I said, 'A little while and you will not see me, and again a little while and you will see me'? Amen, amen, I say to you, you will weep and mourn, while the world rejoices; you will grieve, but your grief will become joy. When a woman is in labor, she is in anguish because her hour has arrived; but when she has given birth to a child, she no longer remembers the pain because of her joy that a child has been born into the world. So you also are now in anguish. But I will see you again, and your hearts will rejoice, and no one will take your joy away from you." (John 16:19-22)

Think about those aspects of your life that you struggle to surrender to God, particularly those things related to your ability to experience joy in your faith life. What pain are you experiencing around those things? Do you have a sense of what God might be trying to birth in you through your surrender? If not, ask the Lord to reveal his purposes for you in those areas.

Here are some additional Scriptures to read prayerfully as you seek the grace of God to be set free from this lie:

- 1 Chronicles 16:27
- Psalm 16:11
- Romans 15:13
- 1 Peter 1:8-9

Spiritual Practice

While the heart of the paschal mystery—giving our lives away so that we might truly gain life—is often opposed to the world's way of thinking, it does have some analogs or "types" that are rooted in our experiences of living in this world. For example, we all have opportunities to invest—either time or money—in something. In other words, we are willing to experience a constraint (that is, "pain") in one area of our life to receive a benefit in another area. Reflect on the times in your life that you have sacrificed time or money in an attempt to receive something greater, and think through your answers to these questions: What was that experience like? Why did you choose to do what you did? What benefit did you receive? Was it worth the sacrifices you made? Given these experiences, what is keeping you from surrendering some of your actions, hobbies, and activities to the Lord?

You might also picture yourself sitting with Jesus and offering him, as gifts, the particular actions and activities that you are worried about surrendering to him. How does Jesus react to each of these gifts? What is he asking you to do with them? What does he want to do with them? Take note of how you respond to what Jesus says and does during this time of imaginative prayer.

Prayer of Renunciation

Heavenly Father, I offer you today my imperfect praise and my half-opened heart. You are the God of truth, and I desire to come to you without excuses or embellishment, simply as I am, lifting up to you my victories and failures, my hopes and fears. You know my struggles, and I ask for the grace of increased trust in your promises.

I renounce and reject the lie that following you will thwart my happiness, and I break any and all inner agreements that I may have made with that lie. By the power of the cross, silence any and all voices in my life that support such a lie, and give me ears to hear your voice, the One who is joy himself.

I ask, Lord, that you would open up a wellspring of joy in my life. Allow it to overflow and spill out of me. Make me a channel of that joy so that as I become more fully who you created me to be, others might encounter the reality of your love for them. I thank you, Father, for being faithful to every one of your promises, and for releasing in me now the freedom you desire for me. I ask all of this in the name of Jesus Christ, your Son.

Invoking the Saints

St. Philip Neri (1515–1595) was born in Florence, the son of a notary. At eighteen years of age he was sent to a live with a kinsman in the town of San Germano, who would make Philip his apprentice and heir. It was there that Philip had his first mystical experience. He then traveled to Rome, taking nothing with him but trusting in God's providence to get him there safely. While in Rome, he began to tutor young students and eventually began studying philosophy and theology as well. Philip showed great promise as a scholar, but, prompted by the call of God, he abruptly gave up his studies and devoted himself to the evangelization of the people of Rome.

It was in this ministry that Philip not only shared the love of God through preaching, but also in service to the poor. In 1544, after a particularly powerful encounter with the Holy Spirit on the eve of Pentecost, his spiritual director persuaded him to consider a vocation to the priesthood. He was ordained in 1551 and eventually founded the Oratorians, a society of priests and brothers bound together by charity and living in service to God and neighbor.

Philip Neri had a lively sense of humor and love of life. It is to this that we can attribute, at least in part, his enormous success in evangelizing people. Philip never shirked from making human connections, even if that meant playing practical jokes on others. He is the only saint we know of who kept a book of jokes near his Bible in his room. He once tweaked the beard of a cardinal whom he declared as being too serious, and reportedly once shaved only half of his own beard to make people laugh. Despite the depth of his devotion to God, Philip found liveliness and joy in living for Jesus, and he shared that joy with all he met—making him a very good companion for those seeking freedom from the lie that following God is a grim calling meant to strip us of all joy.

Chapter Nine

Lie #6: God Is Powerless to Help Me

Hopelessness is a vacuum. It sucks the very air out of life, making it difficult to breathe. It bleeds away willpower, it eats at resolve, and it infects our thinking. If you've ever felt trapped in a situation or overwhelmed by the circumstances of life, you know what that is like. Hope is one of the three theological virtues (the other two being faith and love), and it is the default reality of the kingdom of God. If the Enemy can press into our moments of hopelessness and have us believe that our particular situation—or life in general—is beyond the power of God to change, then we begin to close ourselves off to God and the very real grace that he has made available to us. Once that happens, we become much more vulnerable to Satan's schemes.

This lie—that God is powerless to help us—often begins to manifest when we are in the midst of difficult circumstances that do not seem to have any easy solution. The Accuser will whisper that there is nothing that we can do, and no one we can turn to who will be able to help us—least of all, God. The particulars of our situation start to appear more overwhelming than they actually are, and we can begin to lose perspective. Without anything to counter it, the accusing voice can drown out the voice of our Creator. Prayer becomes difficult, and in this "silence" of God, our sense of alienation and isolation increases.

Sometimes, the hopelessness behind the lie that God is powerless doesn't magnify an external situation, but rather exaggerates the power of our own sinful actions. In other words, we come to believe that what we have done is beyond God's power to redeem. Or that a pattern of sin (what the Church calls a vice) or addiction cannot be broken and brought to healing by God. That its nature is too strong and pervasive for God to handle.

I once met a man—I'll call him Charlie—on a healing retreat. Charlie was middle aged and a successful businessman, father, and husband. He was also addicted to pornography. (As with Jack, in chapter one, this is a common addiction in the Internet age.) Although Charlie had experienced a conversion to Christ and recently returned to the Catholic faith in which he was raised, his addiction to pornography remained. He frequented the Sacrament of Reconciliation, prayed the Rosary, sought counseling, and still struggled with his compulsion to look at pornographic images and videos. In further conversation with him, it was clear that, while he felt guilt for his actions, he did not believe that his actions somehow changed him and made him unlovable to God (Lie #8). Rather, he held a conviction that his decades-long attraction to pornography was too powerful for God to deal with. He even said, "Not even God can help me with this."

It wasn't until later in the retreat, after he witnessed the power of God healing others with similar issues, that Charlie renounced his belief that God was powerless to free him. He then intentionally invited the healing presence of God into his life. The Lord moved deeply within Charlie, and subsequently set him free from his addiction to pornography.

Ultimately, the lie that God is powerless can lead to despair—a state whereby we completely deny the power of God to save us.

Even if we never enter a state of despair, once bound by this lie it becomes harder for us to cooperate with the grace that we receive in Christ. When we believe that our situation is beyond God, we close ourselves off to this grace.

Though this lie is separate from the untrue belief that we were created to suffer (see chapter ten), it is closely related. When we believe the lie that life is suffering, we can easily give in to the lie that God cannot do anything about this suffering. Our faith in God becomes weak and we can conclude that God is either non-existent or irrelevant.

Speaking the Lie

This lie manifests itself in several ways:

- "God cannot do anything about what I am going through."
- "My situation is what it is; I shouldn't hope for anything to change."
- "God might love me, but he certainly can't help me. I'm on my own."
- "Why try to change when I know it will never happen?"
- "What good is God if he won't or can't help me?"
- "I'm never going to get better."

Encountering the Truth

The good news is that hope is the default reality of God's kingdom and we have been received into this kingdom through baptism. For those rooted in Christ, therefore, hope is our horizon—even when we might not be able to see it in our present moment. This hope is grounded not only in God's goodness but in his power to bring life out of death. This is demonstrated most powerfully in the resurrection of Jesus, whereby God takes the most heinous act in human history (the crucifixion of Jesus) and makes it the instrument of our salvation. But the power of God often breaks into everyday life as well, and sometimes in surprising ways.

While speaking at a parish in the southwestern United States, I met a woman named Catherine who asked if I would pray with her. I readily agreed and listened as she recounted a difficult story. She and her husband had been trying to conceive a child for over eight years. They had seen countless specialists, but no one could give them an answer for what might be wrong, and no morally ethical solution had helped at all. Not surprisingly, the stress and pain of their inability to become pregnant placed a strain on their marriage. Furthermore, Catherine had struggled most of her life with anger, and she found that this anger was being directed more and more at her husband.

Catherine had resigned herself to a life without her own biological children and felt a growing distance from a God who, from her perspective, was turning out to be a powerless figment of her imagination. When she first heard me talk about the love of God and his desire to bring healing, Catherine found herself very resistant. But as the day continued, her heart began to soften and she came forward for prayer.

Our prayer time together was fruitful, and just before we were about to end, I felt prompted to pray for an "opening of the womb." Now, that was an odd phrase and new to me, but I dutifully prayed over Catherine using those words. Moved to tears, this young woman thanked me and gave me a hug as we ended our session.

Imagine my surprise when several weeks later I received an email from Catherine. "I'm pregnant" was all it said. I quickly emailed her back and we rejoiced in the goodness and power of God. Nine months later, she gave birth to her beautiful son, Anthony. What's more, the freedom that she experienced because of the healing she received had allowed her and her husband to spend time working through a number of their marital issues. According to Catherine, their marriage was stronger than ever.

Fast forward several years, and Catherine, Anthony, and her husband, Mike, are all doing exceptionally well. Looking back on the experience, Catherine says that this whole journey has brought them all closer to Jesus, and that they are more willing to trust in God's power even when things seem bleak.

Wherever Jesus went in his earthly ministry, he changed hearts and transformed lives, releasing the power of his kingdom—and he still does. Those who have received the indwelling of the Holy Spirit at Baptism *are already walking in the reality of God's kingdom and his power.*

The Letter to the Romans makes this clear: "We are more than conquerors through him who loved us" (Romans 8:37, RSVCE). There is no sin, no pattern of thinking, no addiction, no vice that is beyond God's power to redeem—if we are willing to give our brokenness to the Lord, open our hearts to him, and cooperate with the power that is already ours in him. Likewise, there is no problem, difficulty, tragedy, or trauma that God in his power cannot transform—even death.

This doesn't mean transformation and healing will come easily, or that all problems will cease. It does mean that even in the darkest pit and the deepest pain there is someone who walks with us and to whom pain, suffering, humiliation, grief, and death must yield. The journey may not be without diffi-culty, but the hope which encompasses our horizon, the real-ity of salvation, casts a new light upon it. One that can never be extinguished.

The history of the Church and the lives of the saints give tes-timony to this reality. The weak of this world become strong in him. The worst sinners find in Jesus new life and love. Trans-formed, they become living examples for us.

Understand this. There is nothing you have experienced, no place you have been, nothing that you have done, that is beyond God's power to redeem. Let this truth strengthen you on your journey:

> For God did not give us a spirit of cowardice but rather of power and love and self-control. So do not be ashamed of your testi-mony to our Lord, nor of me, a prisoner for his sake; but bear your share of hardship for the gospel with the strength that comes from God." (2 Timothy 1:7-8)

Unsheathing the Sword of the Spirit

Spend time with the following Scripture passages as you walk through the process of healing from the lie that God is powerless:

- Numbers 23:19
- Isaiah 43:15-19
- Romans 8:10-11
- Romans 8:24-27
- 1 Corinthians 10:13
- 2 Corinthians 4:16-18

Spiritual Practice

Trusting in the Lord's power to help you is essential if you are to grow into the freedom he brings. You can't do this on your own—you've probably tried. What are your expectations regarding the Lord and his work in your life? Take a spiritual inventory noting those things you have hoped and prayed for and where you feel God has failed to deliver. Write down your thoughts and feelings and then review where you stand. Are you speaking of your sense of hopelessness with other Christians so that they can support and encourage you? Are you seeking professional help if that seems necessary? Are there ways you could better dispose yourself to cooperate with God's grace and open yourself more fully to his power? How do your expectations square with the reality that we live in a fallen world?

Take time each day to reflect on how your life could be different if you were truly set free from the lie that God is powerless to help you. Be as specific as possible. What would your days look like? How would you think differently? What would you be able to do that you are not currently able to do? Ask the Lord for strength and perseverance as you seek healing from this lie.

Recognize, too, that the hopelessness behind the lie that God is powerless to help often makes it difficult to ask others for assistance. After all, if God cannot help us, then why bother asking for help from anyone else? But it is a valid spiritual discipline to get help from a friend or from a medical or psychological professional who can guide you in resisting the lie that God cannot set you free. God works through the ordinary course of clinical treatment. The insights of the healing professions wedded to the supernatural action of God can work powerfully to help you on your journey. Don't overlook this option.

Prayer of Renunciation

As you pray through the Scripture passages and engage in spiritual practices to become free of this lie, take time regularly to pray this prayer:

Heavenly Father, at whose command the universe came into being, you who set the stars spinning in the heavens and ordained the lifespan of galaxies, give me the grace to trust in your power. For you, there is no separation between speech and reality. You speak and it is. In the name of Jesus Christ, I renounce and reject any belief that the power of my sin or the struggle I am going through is greater than your power. I bind up all hopelessness through the blood of Jesus Christ and the power of his cross, and I invite you, Holy Spirit, to take possession of my heart. Release in me your fruits and help me to cooperate with the grace you give me. Conform my heart to Jesus, and produce in me the mind of Christ, that I might see the world and my life through the eyes of God's kingdom.

I claim now the promises you have given us in Jesus Christ—that those whom the Son frees are free indeed. I claim that freedom today. Every area of life that is currently in bondage [be as specific as you can here], I submit to your authority, Lord. I ask you to bring your power and freedom to me. I thank you for the deliverance and healing that you are working in me even now. Give me the grace to persevere in this journey of freedom. I ask all of this in the name of Jesus Christ! Amen.

Invoking the Saints

Blessed Bartolo Longo (1841–1926) was an Italian lawyer whose remarkable conversion from Satanism has given hope to many who feel that their own actions or life circumstances place them outside of God's redemptive power. Born to wealthy parents in 1841 in the Italian town of Latiano, he and many of his university friends began to dabble in spiritualism and the occult. After several years of growing immersion, Bartolo became a satanic priest.

Bartolo struggled a great deal during this time with anxiety and depression. At the invitation of a friend, Vincenzo Pepe, Bartolo eventually abandoned Satanism and returned to the practice of his Catholic faith. Even though he developed a strong devotion to the Rosary and eventually became a Dominican Tertiary, Bartolo continued to struggle with anxiety and depression, worried that he would never be set free from the covenants he made with Satan. However, his cooperation with the grace of God deepened his faith and freedom. He was beatified by John Paul II in 1980.

Chapter Ten

Lie #7: I Am Meant to Suffer

All life is suffering. That's not a Christian tenet, by the way. It is one of the Four Noble Truths taught by Buddhism. The second truth is that all suffering arises out of selfish desire, and the third truth is that this desire can be overcome. The fourth and final truth is that one can overcome selfish desire by following the eightfold path of the Buddha.

Why am I writing about the Buddha and his teaching? It's not because I'm recommending Buddhism as a way of life. I mention these foundational teachings of another religion to illustrate the fact that if you take one teaching, let's say the First Noble Truth (all life is suffering) out of context, you can come to the conclusion that living is an inherently negative experience.

Unfortunately, there are many Catholics who would identify with the phrase "all life is suffering" and see it as an important Catholic concept. Life's uncertainty, fragility, and brokenness lead many to believe that suffering is an inherent part of God's design for us on earth. And the devil is happy to facilitate that belief. Life, in this worldview, is an experience of pain, grief, illness, and, ultimately, death, which must be endured. The best we can hope for is that God will give us the grace to endure, to hold out long enough so that we might, at the very end, squeak into purgatory.

In this worldview, pain and suffering are also seen as the default method that God uses to communicate with us. Sherry Weddell, cofounder of the Catherine of Siena Institute and author of *Forming Intentional Disciples: The Path to Knowing and Following Jesus*, often shares the story of one workshop participant who said the following about God: "If it doesn't hurt, how do I know if it's from God?" The idea that God might intend to heal us, free us, or give us grace to transcend our suffering—that the Christian life might be about victory and resurrection in the midst of our suffering—doesn't enter into the thinking of those under the influence of this lie.

Thus, we often grimly support each other with the phrase "offer it up." Although this is a reference to the Church's rich theology of redemptive suffering (which we will explore a bit later), for people trapped by this lie, the phrase "offer it up" is often synonymous with the phrase "suck it up." Good Catholics grit their teeth and march forward, humble enough that they wouldn't dare ask God to free or heal them.

Although the lie that I am meant to suffer is related to the lie that following God means giving up my happiness (Lie #5), they each have a different focus. The giving up of my happiness as a condition of discipleship focuses entirely on God as a competitor to my own joy. The lie that life is wholly about suffering puts the focus on the dreariness and difficulty of this life.

For those who are bound by this lie, Lent is seen as the default season of life. In other words, human existence is supposed to be a lifelong Lent. Any discussion of resurrection and Easter is immediately countered or modified by the phrase, "You can't have resurrection without the cross." Of course, this is absolutely true, but we are not a Lenten people. Our lives are not shaped *only* by the cross. John Paul II said quite the opposite:

"We live in the light of his Paschal Mystery—the mystery of his death *and* resurrection. 'We are an Easter People and Alleluia is our song!'" (Angelus Address, November 30, 1986). The resurrection illuminates the shadow of the cross, shedding light on its horror and in it revealing the triumph of the Father's love over sin, suffering, and death.

This lie, however, can lead us to focus only on the cross in our lives. Under its influence, many Catholics have embraced an inordinate attachment to suffering. Rather than submitting every experience of suffering to the sovereign will of the Lord and the healing power of the Gospel, they unreflectively hold on to suffering without any discernment and can thereby resist the redemptive power of Jesus at work in those experiences.

In his beautiful reflection on human suffering, *Salvifici Doloris*, John Paul II writes:

> And even though the victory over sin and death achieved by Christ in his Cross and Resurrection does not abolish temporal suffering from human life, nor free from suffering the whole historical dimension of human existence, it nevertheless throws a new light upon this dimension and upon every suffering: the light of salvation. (15)

The power of this lie blinds those trapped in its web to the hope which flows from this light of salvation. They often experience life largely as burdensome. This often leads to bitterness, self-hatred, anxiety, depression, and a vulnerability to further attack from the Enemy.

Speaking the Lie

This lie manifests itself in several ways:

- ∞ "Life is about suffering, and God wants me to endure it."
- ∞ "God judges me based on how well I suffer."
- ∞ "Only unfaithful Catholics ask for healing or seek release from suffering."
- ∞ "All I have to help me endure suffering is my human will."
- ∞ "God created me to suffer."
- ∞ "All suffering is from God and should be accepted."
- ∞ "My life is cursed."
- ∞ "Nothing good will ever happen to me."

Encountering the Truth

God created us for a life of fulfillment, peace, and enduring joy—and he wants to give this rich life to us. The reality of suffering in this world is not a feature of God's perfect plan. God did not create us to suffer. John Paul II said it this way:

Thus, the reality of suffering prompts the question about the essence of evil: what is evil? This question seems, in a certain sense, inseparable from the theme of suffering. The Christian response to it is different, for example, from the one given by certain cultural and religious traditions which hold that existence is an evil from which one needs to be liberated. Christianity proclaims the essential *good of existence* and the good of that which exists, acknowledges the goodness of the Creator and proclaims the good of creatures. Man suffers on account of evil, which is a certain lack, limitation or distortion of good.

> We could say that man suffers *because of a good* in which he does not share, from which in a certain sense he is cut off, or of which he has deprived himself. He particularly suffers when he ought—in the normal order of things—to have a share in this good and does not have it. (*Salvifici Doloris*, 7)

We suffer precisely because we are supposed to have this experience of communion, but the fall has separated us from the One for whom we were made. Apart from him, illness, sin, suffering, and death have dominated humanity's existence. However, the immeasurable depth of the Father's love cannot be exhausted. He sends his Son, Jesus, to make a way for us. Looking closely at the ministry of Jesus, we can see the Father's attitude toward suffering in the way that Jesus taught and prayed.

A surface examination of the New Testament could lead us to believe that Jesus commands us to embrace every kind of suffering. We hear Jesus say "take up your cross and follow me," and unless we examine this statement in the broader context of the whole New Testament and the mission of the Church, we can start to believe that the Father really must desire suffering. A closer inspection of Scripture, however, reveals something else.

The gospel writers clearly depict two kinds of suffering. One type of suffering is connected to the cost of discipleship—this include persecution, physical and emotional torment by others, the pain of dying to self and living for others, the hardships of living the Gospel. According to author and Scripture scholar Mary Healy, "When Jesus says 'take up your cross' and exhorts His disciples to expect suffering and rejoice in it, he is referring to the trials associated with persecution for the gospel's sake." Healy calls this kind of suffering "apostolic suffering."

There is another kind of suffering that Jesus encounters in Scripture—the suffering that comes from living in a fallen world, namely illness, demonic torment, and death. Jesus' actions in the context of these sufferings are instructive. Though he urges us to embrace apostolic suffering, his response to illness, demonic torment, and death is healing, exorcism, and resurrection. If suffering was truly intended by God to be a fundamental part of human life, why would he send his Son, Jesus? Why would the Son of God reach out and open the blind eye or heal the lame? Why would he see it as a fundamental part of his messianic mission (see Luke 4:16-21)? And why would he give us two sacraments—Reconciliation and the Anointing of the Sick—whose whole purpose is to bring healing?

Suffering is clearly a part of the human experience because of the fall, but the life of the Father's anointed one, his Christ, proclaims a message of hope, healing, restoration, and change—even in the midst of great suffering. Therefore, *there may be crosses we are holding onto that Jesus never intended for us to carry.* If we allow the lie that we are "meant to suffer" to have power in our lives, we will never hand those crosses over to the Lord for him to do with as he wills.

God's desire and nature is to heal, and we know this by the testimony of Scripture and the lived history of the Church. Sometimes, the Lord changes our hearts, brings inner healing and freedom, and this can change our whole experience of suffering. This happened in my own life, when the Lord set me free from self-hatred and shame and completely changed my experience of living with a disability. Even though the Lord never brought physical healing, I was transformed.

Sometimes, though, the Lord brings physical healing. He changes our suffering, and this change can transform our hearts. Sometimes, he does both. But he always does something! Quite often, walking with someone else along a journey of healing means helping them see the unexpected ways that God has already brought healing.

What of redemptive suffering, then? Am I somehow saying that being a Christian means avoiding suffering, or that Jesus will automatically make everything better in our lives? Of course not. We must understand, however, that suffering is not, by itself, a good. In the context of the mission of the Redeemer, suffering has been transformed. When we unite our suffering with that of Jesus, it is no longer meaningless—it has purpose, and he can use that suffering for the good of others. "Those who share in the sufferings of Christ," John Paul II writes, "preserve in their own sufferings a *very special particle of the infinite treasure* of the world's Redemption, and can share this treasure with others" (*Salvifici Doloris*, 27).

Inner freedom and spiritual maturity, however, allow us to come before the Lord with our suffering in an attitude of self-offering, detachment, and Christian hope. Like my daughter, who when she hurts herself runs to me and cries out, "Daddy, make it better," we can come before the Lord like a little child (see Matthew 18:3) and cry out to the One who created us for healing. We know that in the mysterious working of his will, he desires our ultimate good. Trusting his Father's heart in the midst of the mystery of our suffering, we know that he will work things out for our good (cf. Romans 8:28). If we remain with him in that experience, the power of God's kingdom will be released within us, and we will truly know healing, freedom, peace, and joy.

After all, we were created for those things.

Unsheathing the Sword of the Spirit

As a way of reflecting on the goodness of this life, take your time and prayerfully read through the first chapter of the Book of Genesis. As you progress through the Creation story, note or circle any words or phrases that catch your attention or stir a memory, thought, or emotion. You may want to spend time with these other Scriptures as you walk through the process of healing from the lie that you are "meant to suffer":

- Psalm 23
- John 10:9-10
- 2 Corinthians 1:3-4

Spiritual Practice

Reclaiming a sense of the goodness of this life and the goodness of our Creator are essential in any journey of healing and freedom from the power of this lie. A simple practice that many have found helpful is to intentionally delight in God and the good things that he sends. Of course, spiritual maturity allows us to praise the Lord in every life circumstance, but this lie often causes us to focus on the negative. This practice deliberately shifts our attention to the truth of who God is and his purposes for us. Though we may find that this requires a lot of effort and discipline, particularly at the beginning, if we stay with it the Holy Spirit will come to our aid and help us see with new eyes.

To begin this practice, simply find something that you enjoy—an activity or an experience (eating good food, for example) and make a conscious decision to engage in it more thoughtfully, taking the time to savor what you are experiencing. As you do this, remember to offer thanks and praise to God for the goodness of this experience.

Prayer of Renunciation

Heavenly Father, I thank you for the gift of life, for calling me and sustaining me in being. I thank you, God, for every breath and heartbeat, and I ask for the grace to see every moment of this existence as a gift from you. In the name of your Son, Jesus, I break the authority of every judgment, belief, and pattern of thinking that is rooted in the lie that I am meant to suffer or that this life is only about suffering. I claim the fruits of your Holy Spirit, especially joy. I ask that you would release joy within me and allow me to see the whole of my life experience in the context of your purposes for me. Give me the grace to open my heart to the Father's heart, trusting in his goodness. I ask this in the name of Jesus Christ. Amen.

Invoking the Saints

"You ask me whether I am in good spirits. How could I not be, so long as my trust in God gives me strength? We must always be cheerful. Sadness should be banished from all Christian souls. For suffering is a far different thing from sadness, which is the worst

disease of all. It is almost always caused by lack of faith. But the purpose for which we have been created shows us the path along which we should go, perhaps strewn with many thorns, but not a sad path. Even in the midst of intense suffering it is one of joy."
Blessed Pier Giorgio Frassati (1901–1925)

Pier Giorgio Frassati was born in Turin, Italy in 1901. Frassati developed a relationship with Christ at an early age, and this relationship influenced his whole life. For example, he wanted to become a mining engineer so that he could serve Christ among the miners. A great lover of the goodness of life, Pier Giorgio enjoyed art, theater, and literature, and he especially loved spending time climbing mountains. He deeply appreciated the gift of life and often expressed his gratitude to God in the way he related to others. His friends, for example, would call him an explosion of joy.

This joy remained undimmed even as he served the poor and those who were ill, and it was a hallmark of his life even through the illness that led to his death at the age of twenty-four.

Chapter Eleven

Lie #8: I Am So Broken or Damaged that God Does Not Want to Save Me

Shame on you!

Do you hear what is happening when we use that phrase? It's almost like a curse. When somebody has wronged us (or just done wrong in general), we let that phrase fly—and in doing so thrust shame upon them, like some kind of weight or ungodly burden. When we do that, people often internalize the message and take that burden of shame upon themselves.

Shame is more than guilt. In our postmodern society we look upon guilt as something entirely negative. And yet, guilt can be a powerful way in which the Holy Spirit works through our conscience to let us know that we are not walking down the right path. Shame is something much more insidious and malignant; it is a cancerous weapon that the Enemy uses to break down our self-understanding. We then cut ourselves off from God's love and mercy based on our own judgment of who and what we really are. Here's how it works: Guilt says I've *made* a mistake. Shame says I *am* a mistake.

Do you see the difference?

The Enemy wants to bind us in shame. We all make mistakes— some of them sinful. Often, Satan places temptations before us and encourages us to rationalize why giving in to a particular temptation wouldn't actually be a sin for us. Then, if we end up yielding to that temptation, he takes a step back and begins to accuse us. It's as if he says, "Oh, man . . . I can't believe you actually did that. God will never forgive you for that. And even if he did, if you confess this to a priest, he is going to judge you." The Enemy piles on the weight of shame, wearing down our defenses until we eventually yield to temptation again.

I've heard it put this way: The Enemy knows your name—and chooses to call you by your sin! Why does he do that? Because Satan wants us to fall into the lie of believing that we are what we have done wrong (or what has been done to us). If he can do that, then he truly has us wrapped in shame.

This sense of shame is what empowers the lie that our brokenness makes God unwilling to save us. Unlike the lie rooted in God's powerlessness to save us (Lie #6), this lie causes us to focus on our own unworthiness. In a sense, we become so blinded by disgust and even self-hatred that we decide for God what his reaction to us will be. This lie can also bring with it an accusing voice that speaks into our hearts, reminding us that we are "no good," "stupid," "not deserving of love." This can lead to acts of self-sabotage professionally and personally, self-harm, isolation, bitterness, depression, anxiety, and despair. When this lie binds us, we sometimes have difficulty receiving love, affirmation, intimacy, and even compliments from other people.

The pervasiveness of the lie that our brokenness causes God to close his heart to us can lead us to hear the truth through a filter of shame. For example, the classic summation of the gospel message from John 3:16 "For God so loved the world that he gave his only Son, so that everyone who believes in him might not perish but might have eternal life" becomes "For God so loved the world—except me—that he gave his only Son, so that everyone—except me—who believes in him might not perish but might have eternal life." From this perspective, it's not that God is a bad father (Lie #1), it's that we are such broken and difficult children that he would never want to love us.

And it doesn't have to be our own sinful actions that lead us into the bondage of this lie. The brokenness of others can affect us as well. This is never more true than in the case of abuse, where victims not only end up blaming themselves for what happened to them, but they also believe themselves to be damaged to such an extent that they do not deserve love of any kind—especially from God.

Speaking the Lie

The person bound by this lie usually doesn't doubt the power of God to set them free, heal them, or love them. They simply doubt his desire to do so. This lie manifests itself in several ways:

- ∞ "God does not love me because of what I have done or what has been done to me."
- ∞ "I don't deserve love."
- ∞ "God made me broken."
- ∞ "I am broken or tainted because of what I have done."
- ∞ "I am what I have done (or what has been done to me)."
- ∞ "God's love is for everyone, but not really for me."
- ∞ "I have messed up God's plan for my life."
- ∞ "I deserve to be punished."
- ∞ "If they knew the real me, people wouldn't like me."
- ∞ "I'll never amount to anything."
- ∞ "Nothing good will ever happen to me."

Encountering the Truth

The Father delights in you!

Perhaps this seems like a much more shocking statement than "God loves you." Many of us think about the love of God in a kind of theoretical way. God's love is an essential "law" of the universe, much like gravity. Gravity affects our lives every single day, even at the molecular level, and yet it is an impersonal physical law. We usually never think about it in a personal or intimate way—unless we are falling!

God's loves affects our lives every single day, in the most personal and intimate ways, yet we hardly ever recognize this reality. So, the phrase "God loves you" passes our lips and our ears without much impact.

But the reality that the Father *delights* in you is much more intimate, in your face, and personally challenging. The Father's delight is not abstract. For the Father to delight in me, he must see me, and he must know me; he must be radically involved with the details of my life. And this is exactly what Scripture testifies. "Before I formed you in the womb," the Lord says to the prophet Jeremiah, "I knew you" (Jeremiah 1:5). We can easily gloss over the radical nature of this proclamation. The knowledge of the Lord is not surface knowledge, or the knowledge of an acquaintance. God's knowledge penetrates to the deepest parts of who we are. The Lord knows what will fulfill our desires. He knows what will fill us with joy, and move us to take action against injustice. He knows our strongest fears and can read the desires of our heart.

And as he reveals in his Word, he has known this before we were even conceived. God has always been. There was never a time when he was not. Therefore, his knowledge of us has always existed. God knew us from eternity. That is why I can clearly see the Father dancing for joy at the moment of our conception and saying, "At last, you are here. I have waited for you from before time began. And now, you can receive my love and offer love back in return!"

Think about that: from the moment of your conception, the Father has gazed upon you with love. Not because you have done anything worthwhile, or believed the right things, or kept yourself spotless—but simply because you are the work of his hands, his creation. Not to get too philosophical, but God loves us simply because we exist, and we exist simply because God loves us.

I remember the first time I saw my daughter, Siena, as my wife gave birth. She was fragile, bloodied from her journey into the world, and indescribably beautiful. My heart flooded with a fierce and overwhelming love from the first moment I gazed upon her. Siena didn't have to work for that love. I wasn't unsure of my heart until she proved herself. It was an experience of immediate, life-changing love. That love comes from the Father's heart. If I, who am filled with imperfection, can have this experience of my daughter, how much more does God, who is perfect love, love us?

Jesus says something similar in the Gospel of Luke:

And I tell you, ask and you will receive; seek and you will find; knock and the door will be opened to you. For everyone who asks, receives; and the one who seeks, finds; and to the one who knocks, the door will be opened. What father among you would hand his son a snake when he asks for a fish? Or hand him a scorpion when he asks for an egg? If you then, who are wicked, know how to give good gifts to your children, how much more will the Father in heaven give the Holy Spirit to those who ask him?" (11:9-13)

And as the apostle Paul declared:

What will separate us from the love of Christ? Will anguish, or distress, or persecution, or famine, or nakedness, or peril, or the sword? . . . No, in all these things we conquer overwhelmingly through him who loved us. For I am convinced that neither death, nor life, nor angels, nor principalities, nor present things, nor future things, nor powers, nor height, nor depth, nor any other creature will be able to separate us from the love of God in Christ Jesus our Lord. (Romans 8:35, 37-39)

Nothing we have done (or that has been done to us) is a barrier to God and his will to save us. The voice of this lie, however, will try to convince us otherwise. In fact, some of you who have been reading through this chapter may be wrestling with a voice inside of you that is listing all the reasons that this truth doesn't apply to you. The voice of accusation and condemnation sometimes shouts when the truth gets too near. But Paul rebukes that voice in an earlier passage from Romans:

What then shall we say to this? If God is for us, who can be against us? He who did not spare his own Son but handed him over for us all, how will he not also give us everything else along with him? Who will bring a charge against God's chosen ones? It is God who acquits us. Who will condemn? It is Christ [Jesus] who died, rather, was raised, who also is at the right hand of God, who indeed intercedes for us. (8:31-34)

God is undeniably for us. The proof is the presence of Jesus Christ in human history. If God did not hold back his only Son, if he offered his Son for our sake, then he wouldn't hold back all that comes with Jesus. Yes, this includes his teaching, his example, and his death—but it also includes everything that flows from his death, which is his resurrection, ascension, and the gift of his Holy Spirit.

The Enemy, however, wants to bind this reality of the Father's love and Jesus' sacrifice with lies. Satan's ultimate strategy is to have us view the cross as a proclamation of our sinfulness. He wants us to look upon the cross and to bind us in shame saying "Look what *you've* done to him! How could God ever love you after doing that to him?"

But the truth is altogether different. There is nothing that you have done, there is no thought you've ever had, there is no tragedy or trauma that you have experienced that can ever change the Father's heart for you. It is constant, and unchanging. God has saved you, not because you are good, but because *he* is good. And that goodness is everlasting.

So, do not be afraid to run to him. Open your heart and receive his goodness. Come just as you are, broken and battered, angry and uncertain, weighed down by life and by the choices you've made. There is new life waiting for you, rest and relief, and a love that can never, ever be swayed.

Come.

Unsheathing the Sword of the Spirit

Spend time reading Romans 5:6-11 as you walk through the process of healing from the lie that your brokenness makes God unwilling to love you. Take time to reflect on what this passage means by the phrase "enemies" of God (5:10). Would you consider yourself an enemy of God? If so, why? How does God treat his enemies according to this Scripture verse? What would have to happen for you to feel reconciled to God? How would you react if those things did happen?

Here are some other passages that you might want to pray through:

- Zephaniah 3:17
- John 15:12-16
- Romans 8:31-39
- Ephesians 2:4-7
- Revelation 21:3-4

Spiritual Practice

In your prayer times over the next week, ask the Lord to reveal to you those specific incidences, memories, and past actions that are weighing you down with shame. Then imagine yourself taking each one of these specific experiences and offering it to the Lord. You might find it helpful to place one hand over your heart and the other hand on your leg in front of you. Then, physically pull each memory or experience out of your heart and place it in the palm of the hand on your leg in front of you. When you are finished, place the hand that is over your heart underneath the hand on your leg, then lift both hands right up in the air and imagine that you are tossing these memories and past experiences to the Lord. If you find it helpful, you can also include in this exercise any words of accusation or shame that you have heard internally or through someone else.

When you are ready, immediately follow up this exercise with the prayer of renunciation below.

Prayer of Renunciation

Heavenly Father, I thank you for creating me and calling me into new life in Jesus Christ. Lord, you know the desires of my heart and the course of my life. You know what I have experienced—my victories and my triumphs, my joys and my grief. I believe that nothing can separate me from your life, and that my identity does not depend on what I have done, or what has been done to me, but rather rests only on your love for me.

I declare your love over my life today and receive it with an open heart. And so, Father, I ask that you take these experiences of shame from me. I offer them to you freely, and in the name of Jesus Christ, I break their power, influence, and authority in my life. Unite these wounds with the wounds of your Son on the cross. And in exchange, pour forth new life, kingdom life, in me! I thank you, Father, for the freedom and healing you are bringing me now. I love you, Lord, and desire to give you my whole heart—even if I have no idea what that might mean at this time in my life.

Lord Jesus, you have called me back to the Father, and I declare that you are the Lord of my life. I acknowledge my sinfulness and humbly come before your throne of mercy. I am yours—a child of the Most High God. Teach me to love and to become even more fully what you have created me to be.

I ask this in your most precious, most glorious name— Jesus Christ!

Invoking the Saints

"This morning my soul is greater than the world since it possesses you, you whom heaven and earth do not contain." St. Margaret of Cortona (1247–1297)

Margaret was born in Loviana, in the Tuscany region of Italy, in 1247. Her mother died when Margaret was young and her stepmother had little love for the willful, free-spirited daughter that came with her marriage to Margaret's father. Receiving no welcome at home, Margaret ran away with a young man from another town and bore him a son out of wedlock. When her lover was murdered nine years later, she was forced to return to her father's house as a penitent. Unfortunately, her father refused to accept Margaret and her son, and she found asylum with the Friars Minor in Cortona.

Although she encountered the Lord Jesus and gave her life to him, Margaret continued to struggle with sins of the flesh. Overcome with shame at her past actions, she attempted to mutilate her face, but was stopped by a Franciscan Friar named Giunta. She soon joined the Third Order Franciscans and grew close to Jesus in prayer. She devoted her life to nursing those who were ill—especially the poor and destitute. Throughout her life as a disciple she received messages from Jesus, some of which Friar Giunta recorded.

Weighed down as she was by her own past and the humiliation of knowing how far away she was from Christ in her younger days, nevertheless Margaret was able to lean into the mercy of Jesus and allow the Lord's grace to transform her. She is a friend to those who struggle to come to terms with their shame and brokenness.

Chapter Twelve

Lie #9: I Have to Be Perfect (or Nearly So) to Earn God's Love

Our culture places a high value on productiveness—on what individuals contribute to society.

This is such a major focus that we often view people who do not produce anything as possessing less value. We see this clearly in how we treat the elderly, infirm, and unborn. In short, respect and deference are given to the degree that one does something worthwhile. Unfortunately, this attitude can infect our relationship with God if we are not careful.

Here's how. The Enemy is quick to capitalize on any leanings we have to judge someone—including ourselves—according to what they accomplish. Often, those who have experienced either one or both parents as judgmental or having exceptionally high standards or as never being satisfied can grow up with the idea that affirmation only follows when they meet expectations or do things perfectly. If the family system also lacked external signs of affection, it's likely that such a performance-based dynamic was present.

The Enemy's strategy here is to get us to transfer this image of a demanding parent to God. Under the effects of this lie, we come to see God as a cold, impersonal, distant judge who weighs every "jot and tittle" of our lives against his infinite perfection. In this worldview, God only offers his approval, love, salvation, healing, and presence to those who follow him perfectly. As the devil is quick to point out, we will never be able to follow him perfectly. This lie can lead us into a kind of "performance Christianity," whereby we see ourselves as needing to earn God's love—and perennially falling short. Ironically, in believing that our salvation is almost entirely up to us, we experience a profound sense of powerlessness.

Those who suffer under the effects of this lie often feel a tremendous pressure to get things right. Every failure, every sin, every imperfection can bring with it a heightened sense of fear and a sometimes-overwhelming sense of guilt. Often, in this worldview, there is a struggle with releasing control and a niggling but very real pattern of self-judgment, self-hatred, or shame that lurks behind and beneath our thoughts.

There is another facet to this lie that can lead to a pattern of presumption and lethargy in relation to God's love and our salvation. This aspect of the lie says that if we can earn God's love through what we do, then simply doing religious things (attending Mass, praying, participating in devotions) will be enough to "get us to heaven," regardless of our inner disposition and relationship to Christ. In its extreme progression, this lie can lead us to believe that God will let us into heaven because we are basically good people. In this worldview, what Jesus has to do with our salvation is unclear.

Unfortunately, Catholics seem particularly vulnerable to this perspective. In our desire to distinguish ourselves from our Protestant brothers and sisters who profess a "faith alone" approach to salvation, we tend to emphasize the role of good works in salvation. But this "good works" approach is inadequate. Poor catechesis over the last seventy years has produced generations of Catholics who are ignorant of the saving action of Jesus Christ and are unfamiliar with the Bible, prayer, and the interior life. As a result, many Catholics today are functional semi-Pelagians, "earning" their way to heaven. Pelagius was an early fifth-century theologian who taught, among other things, that we do not need grace to take steps toward salvation; we can do it by our own effort.

People bound by a belief that they must be perfect in order to earn God's love can end up substituting religious activity for a relationship with God. Ask Catholics if they have a relationship with Jesus and they will often respond, "Of course, I go to Mass." Now, is it true that at the celebration of every Mass, we can experience the most intimate aspects of a relationship with God as we receive him in the Eucharist? Of course. But once again we must say that the sacraments are not magical. We must come to them with an intentionality and an openness of heart. Just doing Catholic things does not guarantee salvation. Furthermore, one of the signs of an authentic relationship with God is the growing desire to develop that relationship in all areas of life, not just in the fulfilment of religious obligations.

That's why this lie is so critical to the Enemy's strategy!

Speaking the Lie

There are numerous ways that this lie manifests itself in our lives:

- "If I'm not perfect, God won't love me."
- "God's judgment on my life is negative, but I can change his mind if I act right."
- "My salvation is up to me."
- "God loves me because I'm good."

∾ "God saves me because I'm good."

∾ "I don't deserve love or affection if I haven't earned it."

∾ "God might be love, but I have to do the right things for him to offer love to me."

Encountering the Truth

St. Thérèse of Lisieux once said, "Everything is grace." What a perfect summation of the truth that unravels this particular lie. Grace is not so much a thing as it is a reality—grace is the very life of God. Everything that *is*, then, comes from the very life of God. This includes saving faith. Paul talks about it this way: "For by grace you have been saved through faith, and this is not from you; it is the gift of God" (Ephesians 2:8). Salvation is a gift offered to every human person, and we access this gift through faith in Jesus Christ. It is Jesus who invites us into this salvific relationship, and so even faith itself is a gift. The Church teaches that "*Faith is a gift of God, a supernatural virtue infused by him*" (CCC 153).

This doesn't mean that faith is merely God pulling our strings and making us some kind of holy automatons. Love cannot be coerced, and therefore we must do our part. St. Augustine said that "God created us without us, but he did not will to save us without us" (see *CCC* 1847). The *Catechism* acknowledges this and also calls faith an "authentically human act" (154). Moved by the grace of God, the intellect and will cooperate with this grace and we are therefore transformed.

Why is this kind of distinction and clarity important? Because it helps us realize that faith's power is located in God and not in us. Sure, our assent and cooperation are essential in releasing the salvific power of God in our lives; however, the transforming power of faith does not come from us, but the Lord. This means we are not the cause of our salvation, and therefore, salvation does not depend on our perfection, but on the perfect love of God.

If anyone is saved in the world—whether they are Christian, Jewish, Muslim, atheist, or of any philosophy—they are ultimately saved only because of Jesus. "There is no salvation through anyone else," Scripture attests, "nor is there any other name under heaven given to the human race by which we are to be saved" (Acts 4:12).

Therefore, we must realize that no one deserves to be saved, or to enter into heaven, just because they are good. Paul calls out the truth that "all have sinned and are deprived of the glory of God" (Romans 3:23). It is only through the actions of Christ—his life, death, resurrection, and ascension—that we can be saved. There is nothing that you and I can do that will make God love us even more than he already does right now! No number of daily Masses, Rosaries, charitable works, Bible study sessions, prayers, or good deeds changes God's mind or heart about us.

Am I saying that attending Mass, praying the Rosary, reading Scripture, and so forth are without merit and power? Certainly not! When we do these things and engage in the life of a disciple with the proper disposition, it changes our heart. God's grace works in us and allows us to receive even more of his life and, therefore, become like him.

If there is nothing we can do to make God love us even more, then the reverse is also true. There is nothing that you and I can do that would make him love us any less! He meets us right where we are, and he loves us for who we are right now. Not for what we may one day become, or what we have been in the past. But in the here and now. His love is eternally present to us, simply because he is love.

You don't need to perform for that love. Perfection is not a precondition to receiving his love—and neither is holiness. He loves you right where you are, and he longs to bring you into the center of his Sacred Heart.

Today.

All it takes is your *yes*.

Unsheathing the Sword of the Spirit

As you pray through the following Scriptures, take time to reflect on what the Bible means when it mentions the word "believe."

- John 3:16
- John 5:24
- Acts 10:43
- Acts 13:38-39

Spiritual Practice

It is one thing to understand that some Catholics see their faith through a semi-Pelagian lens, and another to know where we fall into that pattern of thinking ourselves. As part of the spiritual practice geared toward freedom from this lie, map out the areas in your life where you feel that you need to be perfect. One way to zero in on these areas is to take note of where you might be experiencing significant fear or frustration, and then ask the Lord to reveal what might be behind those emotions. Do this especially for your relationship with God. If it helps, write down these areas of fear and frustration and continue to take them to prayer. As you pray the renunciation prayer below, specifically rebuke and renounce those things. Invite the Lord into those particular places and ask him for strength and renewal.

Prayer of Renunciation

Heavenly Father, I praise you for the glory and power of your divine life, and I thank you for wanting me to share in it. Today, give me the grace of stillness—still all the desire within me to prove my love to you and still all oppressive and fearful thoughts that I shall never be able to do so. I renounce and reject the lie that I must earn your love, and I rebuke all thought patterns, compulsions, and fears that flow from this lie. I ask also that you would deafen me to the voice of the Accuser and consecrate my ears so that I might only hear your voice—the voice of the Good Shepherd.

I profess now my utter inability to save myself or to increase your love for me in any way solely through my own actions. I lay down now any fear of giving up control, and I turn my life over to your Son, Jesus. Renew within me the reality of your love and the power of the Holy Spirit. Allow me to more openly cooperate with the work of the Spirit in my life. I thank you for the freedom, peace, and joy that you are already bringing to fruition in me, and I thank you for your saving help. I ask all of this in the name and presence of Jesus Christ. Amen.

Invoking the Saints

> "Do you realize that Jesus is there in the tabernacle expressly for you—for you alone? He burns with the desire to come into your heart. . . Don't listen to the demon, laugh at him, and go without fear to receive the Jesus of peace and love."
> St. Thérèse of Lisieux (1873–1897)

One of the most popular saints in modern times, St. Thérèse was born in Alençon, France. A headstrong but pious child, she experienced a life-changing moment of grace when she was fourteen, and soon after entered the Carmelite convent in Lisieux. Though she struggled with illness throughout her short life, and often wrestled with dark nights of doubt, Thérèse persevered with a childlike trust in the love and providence of God. Through that trust, she never let her moments of doubt or her failures convince her that God didn't love her. She offered those doubts and failures to God, understanding that she was his beloved daughter despite all of her imperfections.

Thérèse saw her mission in life as helping the world fall in love with God and she offered herself in prayer to that end. She knew that she would be an even more powerful instrument of the Lord's grace after her death and said: "I will spend my heaven doing good on earth. I will let fall a shower of roses." She was canonized by Pope Pius XI in 1925, and St. John Paul II declared this "flower" of the Lord a Doctor of the Church in 1997.

The abandonment that Thérèse demonstrated throughout her life, and the trust she had in God's grace, make her a wonderful companion and prayer partner for those struggling to free themselves from the effects of the lie that we must be perfect in order to earn God's love.

Chapter Thirteen

Lie #10: I Am Insignificant

Have you ever played hide-and-seek? When I was younger, I loved hide-and-seek—it was my "go-to" game and one that my friends and I especially enjoyed on our block during the summers in Long Island. One time, I remember playing this game with my older cousins at a family gathering—I was around six or seven years old. After finding what I thought was a great space to hide, I sat down and waited for someone to find me.

And waited. And waited. And waited.

You get the idea.

After what felt like ages to my younger self (and was probably only ten minutes or so), I bravely ventured forth from my space to see what was happening—only to find that my cousins had already stopped playing the game and were on to something else. I realized in that moment that I didn't really matter to my older cousins, at least not in the context of playing silly kids' games (we were actually pretty close).

While I have never really struggled with the effects of the lie that I am insignificant, I have never forgotten what my experience that day felt like. I was invisible. And that experience of invisibility, of not mattering at all, sits at the heart of this lie. This sense of insignificance isn't primarily about isolation or shame, but of personal powerlessness. Of course, each of these ten lies is a doorway for the others, but those who struggle with the lie of insignificance wrestle with a poverty rooted in their identity and a "smallness" that they see as a part of who they are. They may not feel ashamed of themselves, and they may also acknowledge that they have real gifts and talents, but they believe that these gifts are irrelevant in the circumstances in which they find themselves, or are unimportant enough that others fail to see them or their gifts.

Those who struggle with this lie may have given up on trying to be noticed or making their mark on the world. They bury their gifts or passively sit in the background, convinced that they don't matter. They might quietly go about their lives with a pervasive sense of sadness, bitterness, and anger that serves as an obstacle to their relationship with God and others. This lie may also drive people to engage in a pattern of extreme actions and activities in an attempt to get others to notice them. These acts may include things that are harmful both to themselves and to others.

Please note that I am not talking about the characteristics of introversion here, or someone who is simply quietly competent by nature. Introversion is a personality trait and by itself is not a dysfunction or a problem. But this lie that *I am insignificant* brings with it a destructive way of seeing oneself—in its extreme manifestations, it can lead someone to believe that they don't belong anywhere or that they should be dead.

The Enemy also likes to dress this lie up in the language of humility. As Catholics, we know that we should be both faithful and humble. True humility, however, is not the belief that we are insignificant or invisible or don't matter. Authentic humility means that we live out who we are created to be without attaching undue significance to our gifts or abilities.

Speaking the Lie

There are numerous ways that this lie manifests itself in our lives:

- ∞ "I feel like I am invisible."
- ∞ "I don't belong here."
- ∞ "I shouldn't be here."
- ∞ "I don't matter."
- ∞ "I can't say no; I have to let others do whatever they want."
- ∞ "No one will ever believe me."
- ∞ "No one needs me."
- ∞ "I have nothing to offer anyone."
- ∞ "Nobody cares if I live or die."

Encountering the Truth

You are probably recognizing a pattern right now—God's response to this lie is the incarnation, death, and resurrection of his Son, Jesus. In Jesus, the Lord draws near to us; he truly is Emmanuel, the God who is *with* us. But the voice of this lie says, "God may have drawn near to humanity, but God is very big, and you are very small, much too small for him to even notice you."

The testimony of God's word, though, proclaims something quite different. Scripture frequently notes the personal and intimate nature of the Lord's love. In Hosea, for example, God says of himself about his wayward people:

I drew them with human cords,
with bands of love;
I fostered them like those
who raise an infant to their cheeks;

I bent down to feed them. (11:4)

In Isaiah we read:

"You are precious in my eyes
and honored, and I love you." (43:4)

To be held as tenderly as an infant, to be precious and honored and loved, is to be known and seen—a far cry from insignificance.

God's personal and intimate love extends to each member of the human race. "Are not two sparrows sold for a small coin?" Jesus asks in Matthew's gospel. "Yet not one of them falls to the ground without your Father's knowledge. Even all the hairs of your head are counted. So do not be afraid; you are worth more than many sparrows" (Matthew 10:29-31). Your life is not invisible to the Lord. His gaze is so intimate that it numbers the hairs on your head.

The Word of God didn't leave the glory of heaven for a nameless, faceless humanity. He didn't hand himself over to be beaten, tortured, and crucified for an idea. When Jesus hung on that cross, his eyes gazed upon you, upon the winding track of your life. When he was laid in the tomb, he held your sins in its silent embrace. And after his resurrection from the dead and his ascension, he carried your name into the heart of Trinitarian love. This fulfills what the prophet Isaiah proclaimed many years before the coming of Christ: "See, upon the palms of my hands I have engraved you" (49:16).

While leading a parish mission several years ago, I met a woman named Barbara. After just a few minutes of talking with her, it became clear that "Barb" (as she asked me to call her) carried exceptionally heavy burdens. She even looked a bit ragged and harried. When I asked her what was wrong, she nearly wept and said that she wished God could see how much pain she was in. "I feel so small, and my greatest wish is to know that God actually sees me" were her exact words.

I invited her to sit as I listened to her story, and Barb shared with me the difficulties in her life—and there were many. She came from a broken home and left home as soon as she turned eighteen. In the course of her life, she had procured several abortions and given up a child for adoption. Though she was married currently and had two children of her own from that marriage, her history was filled with grief and pain.

At one point, as Barb shared her story, a name came to my mind over and over again. Not really knowing why this was happening, I gently interrupted Barb and asked her what this name (which I can't remember) had to do with her story. As soon as I asked the question, Barb turned white and began to sob. After a quick moment of panic at what I might have done wrong, I asked Barb why she was so upset. She said she wasn't upset. She told me that recently she had attended a Rachel's Vineyard retreat for post-abortive women. On that retreat, they encouraged the participants to give names to the children that they had aborted as part of the healing process. The name which I had shared with Barb was the name that she had given one of her aborted children. She hadn't even shared this information with her husband.

Barb's greatest wish was to know that God saw her, and in that moment the Lord revealed his tender mercy and presence, demonstrating that he not only saw her, but knew intimately the road that she had traveled. He had traveled it with her. Barb's heart opened wide to the Lord that day. We prayed intently after that, and Barb was able to start a new phase in her journey of healing.

The Lord's intimate and personal love has major implications for us. God doesn't see us or love us because we are significant in some way. Rather, we are significant because God sees and loves us. In other words, our value comes from God, and God alone. Because of him, we are never invisible, and we will never truly be overlooked.

To be set free from this lie, begin to see yourself as God sees you, and not as you perceive others seeing you. Recognize that of all the people who have ever lived, and all the people who will ever live, no one can respond to the love and the call of God in their lives exactly as you can. You are an unrepeatable gift that God offers to the world as a sign of his goodness and care.

Become who you are—in Christ!

Unsheathing the Sword of the Spirit

Here are some Scriptures to read prayerfully as you seek God's grace in order to be set free from this lie:

- Job 34:21
- Psalm 33:13-1
- Hebrews 4:12-13
- Matthew 6:25-34

Spiritual Practice

The key to freedom from the lie that *I am insignificant* rests in vision, in growing in our ability to let ourselves be seen and recognized for who we actually are. Reflect on those areas in your life where you feel as if you are invisible. The tricky part of this lie is that we may in fact have areas in our life where we are "seen." We may even be in leadership roles within the family, work, church, or various organizations—and yet we may feel insignificant or invisible in another part of our life. Highlighting these "unseen" areas allows us to focus the light of God's truth on them. In prayer, invite the Spirit of God to illuminate those places so that you can know how God is present in them. Ask him specifically to bring freedom into those areas.

Sometimes the power of this lie blinds us to the actual feedback we may be receiving from others. For example, we may feel insignificant at work, believing that we don't really play a role on the team. And yet, we may be missing the fact that although no one is giving us verbal feedback, every member of the team comes to us to help them solve a problem. Therefore, ask the Lord to open your own eyes and ears so that you can truly receive all the data and know in a deeper way what is actually happening. Extend that prayer to include others who are involved in that area of your life. Ask the Lord to open their eyes to see who you are.

Prayer of Renunciation

Heavenly Father, you who are the source of my life and the foundation of all that is good, praise be to your name in all the earth. I thank you, Lord, for seeing me, for looking upon me from the first moment of my conception, and for sending your Son, that I might truly become your child. I renounce, reject, and rebuke all lies that may have led me to believe that I am insignificant, unnoticed, or invisible—that I don't matter or don't belong.

Today, I claim the inheritance of your kingdom, Lord. I know that my identity does not rest on how other people view me, judge me, or evaluate me. It rests only on your love for me. Give me the grace, Lord, to surrender my heart to that love in Jesus Christ. Help me, Lord, to see myself not as the world sees me, but as you see me, and let me hold that image in my heart. I thank you for the freedom and new life you are already raising up in me, and I ask all of this in the name of your Son, Jesus Christ. Amen.

Invoking the Saints

St. Germaine Cousin (1579–1601) was born to parents of moderate means in the small French village of Pibrac. Her life was marked by a number of challenges right from the start: she suffered with a deformed right hand from birth, as well as a glandular disease known as scrofula that caused abscesses on her neck. She lost her mother at an early age, and her stepmother was exceptionally cruel, banishing Germaine from the household and forcing her to work as a shepherd, ostensibly to protect her other children from catching scrofula. Her bed was in the stable—away from the rest of the family.

Despite being treated as if she wasn't there, Germaine grew up with an incredible sense of the presence of God and devoted herself to following him. She also had a special devotion to Mary. Germaine's piety and love of God were initially met by mild derision from her fellow townsfolk, but it soon became clear to them that the Lord watched over this humble young girl. Whenever she could, she would teach the children of the village about God and serve the poor from her own meager resources. Moved by her faithfulness, Germaine's father eventually forbade his wife from banishing his daughter, but such was Germaine's love of God, that she told her father she wanted to remain in her humbled position. Germaine died when she was twenty-two, and Pope Pius IX canonized her in 1867.

St. Germaine knew intimately the pain of insignificance. Separated from the life of her family and treated as if she didn't exist, she was confident of God's love and care for her, secure in her identity as a daughter of God. Ask her to intercede for you as you journey to freedom from this lie.

Chapter Fourteen

Parting Thoughts

The one who began a good work in you will
continue to complete it until the day of Christ Jesus.
(Philippians 1:6)

The journey of healing is an ongoing process.

It means growing into who we were created to be and drinking more deeply from the chalice of freedom which Jesus offers us. There will be bumps along the way, setbacks and obstacles that maybe we didn't imagine in our wildest dreams. Through it all, we will experience the support of others, the indifference of others, and perhaps even the opposition of others. Certainly, the devil will try to press in, attempting to impede our progress.

That's okay.

This process is a very human one. In reflecting on the Church's mission of accompanying humanity on this journey to salvation, John Paul II acknowledged that "Man is the way for the Church—a way that, in a sense, is the basis of all the other ways that the Church must walk—because man—every man without any exception whatever—has been redeemed by Christ" (*Redemptor Hominis*, 14). This way the Church must walk will, therefore, get messy because human life is messy. Don't get discouraged. Don't let your stumbling, backsliding, and failures lead you to believe another of Satan's lies: that the presence of difficulties in our journey of healing is proof that we are on the wrong path or not making any progress.

God doesn't want to see only a small part of us set free; his desire isn't simply for some of our heart. Rather, the Lord's desire is for our complete healing and wholeness, full restoration of our identity as sons and daughters of the Father, and complete surrender to his Sacred Heart. On a practical level, it means that God is not going to quit on us. He continues to seek us out, call after us, and invite us to experience the Father's love. It doesn't matter how many times we've fallen back into the false worldview of a lie or acted under its influence. The grace of God is always there for us to reach out and grab onto.

This also means that whatever degree of freedom we have experienced up to this point in our life—Jesus has more in store for us. We will never exhaust the capacity that God has to heal and reconcile us to himself and each other. When I received healing and deliverance during an encounter with Jesus Christ while I was in graduate school, that didn't signal the end of my journey. In fact, that encounter launched me on an entirely different journey—a lifetime of discipleship which, in turn, led me to ministry and the Sacrament of Holy Orders as a deacon. During my time in ministry, I have come face-to-face with my own inadequacies, my own limitations, and my own brokenness. In that experience, the Lord has clearly revealed those areas of my life that require further healing and freedom. And that process continues today.

All of us are works in progress, or perhaps it might be better to say that we are saints in training. Your journey into the heart of God's freedom and love will continue long after you put this book down. My prayer is that in these pages you have found food for the journey, a sense of hope, and some practical tools to help you cooperate with God's grace.

In the end, this grace is really all we have—made present in Jesus Christ. May he give you courage and strength to become who you really are in him.

Further Reading

Readers interested in exploring more about spiritual warfare are encouraged to look at the following books:

Abba's Heart: Finding Our Way Back to the Father's Delight by Matthew Lozano and Neal Lozano

Be Healed: A Guide to Encountering the Powerful Love of Jesus in Your Life by Bob Schuchts

Be Transformed: The Healing Power of the Sacraments by Bob Schuchts

Deliverance from Evil Spirits by Francis MacNutt

Healing by Francis MacNutt

Healing: Bringing the Gift of God's Healing to the World by Mary Healy

Interior Freedom by Jacques Philippe

Loved as I Am: An Invitation to Conversion, Healing, and Freedom through Jesus by Miriam James Heidland

Manual for Spiritual Warfare by Paul Thigpen

Unbound: A Practical Guide to Deliverance by Neal Lozano

Unbound Ministry Guidebook: Helping Others Find Freedom in Christ by Matthew Lozano and Neal Lozano

the WORD
among us ®
The *Spirit* of Catholic Living

T his book was published by The Word Among Us. Since 1981, The Word Among Us has been answering the call of the Second Vatican Council to help Catholic laypeople encounter Christ in the Scriptures.

The name of our company comes from the prologue to the Gospel of John and reflects the vision and purpose of all of our publications: to be an instrument of the Spirit, whose desire is to manifest Jesus' presence in and to the children of God. In this way, we hope to contribute to the Church's ongoing mission of proclaiming the gospel to the world so that all people would know the love and mercy of our Lord and grow more deeply in their faith as missionary disciples.

Our monthly devotional magazine, *The Word Among Us*, features meditations on the daily and Sunday Mass readings, and currently reaches more than one million Catholics in North America and another half million Catholics in one hundred countries around the world. Our book division, The Word Among Us Press, publishes numerous books, Bible studies, and pamphlets that help Catholics grow in their faith.

To learn more about who we are and what we publish, visit us at www.wau.org. There you will find a variety of Catholic resources that will help you grow in your faith.

Embrace His Word, Listen to God . . .

www.wau.org